UNBRIDLE
THE
MAGIC WITHIN

UNBRIDLE
THE
MAGIC WITHIN

*How to create
your best life now!*

JIMMY & LORI GUNSCH

TAG

Quantity discounts are available on bulk orders.
Contact sales@TAGPublishers.com for more information.

TAG Publishing, LLC
2618 S. Lipscomb
Amarillo, TX 79109
www.TAGPublishers.com

Office (806) 373-0114
Fax (806) 373-4004
info@TAGPublishers.com

ISBN: 978-1-59930-363-5

First Edition

Copyright © 2011 Jimmy & Lori Gunsch

Cover & Text: Lloyd Arbour, www.tablloyd.com

Cover photo and author photos by:
Krista Haggerty
Head Over Heels Photography
www.headoverheelsphotography.ca

DEDICATION

To everyone who is striving to make a better life for themselves and their families!

and

Jessica & Ashley

You are the inspiration and the courage that keeps us moving forward on our journey!

We love you both very much!

CONTENTS

ONE

STICKS, ROCKS, AND POT HOLES

*"Remember, happiness doesn't depend
on who you are or what you have:
it depends solely on what you think."*

— DALE CARNEGIE
WRITER/LECTURER

CHAPTER 1

Most people spend their entire lives striving for just one thing – happiness. At times it may seem that life is conspiring against you and that happiness is some sort of goal that only other people attain. We are all constantly bombarded by stress at work, trouble with our relationships, and then, of course, there is money. We get to the end of each day just glad we made it through and hope that tomorrow will be better.

So when does this 'happiness' idea kick in? We were guilty, as is most of the population, of thinking that at some point we would arrive at happiness like it is a destination you can buy a ticket too. But that's not true. Happiness is wrapped up in the *journey of life* and has no bearing on what you do or don't do, what you have, who you are with, or what your personal career status may be. It is very easy to assume that if a particular event happens, you will be happy; but inevitably, when that event happens, life continues just as it always has and the idea of happiness morphs into something different. It is normal and good to have different dreams and desires as you age and travel through life. What you thought would make you happy when

you were 20 years old and single is certainly very different from your idea of happiness when you are 35 and married with a family.

The good news is that no matter your stage or circumstance in life you can *choose* to be happy. Happiness isn't something you stumble into; it is something you *choose* each and every day. Does this mean you won't have troubles with coworkers, get caught up in bad circumstances, or have family members diagnosed with a disease? NO. There will always be challenges to deal with, but how you *choose* to face these challenges and issues will determine your happiness.

Jimmy has been involved in rodeo and ranching since childhood. There is no doubt that his experiences in this environment have added to his deep commitment and work ethic. Our whole family has benefited from the camaraderie of other families who had cattle and worked close to the land. But a few years ago, while in a roping competition, Jimmy was involved in an unavoidable accident in one of the rodeo events he participated in. This accident is uncommon but it does occur occasionally in the sport. Though Jimmy was well respected as a top competitor, many in the governing organization found it easier to blame him for the incident.

To be honest, we were baffled! Suddenly, years of hard work and honest dealing with people was pushed aside by a few trying to make Jimmy a scapegoat. We easily could have shrunk away from the controversy and been very unhappy. Instead we chose to stand up to the controversy and were secure in knowing that we did the right thing. It was hard, but what we discovered was that you can never expect other people's opinions to make you happy.

We now know how temporary and fleeting people's opinions are in life. We learned that if you know that you are behaving in a way that is consistent with your beliefs you can achieve happiness no matter the circumstances.

You can *choose* to move on and create your own life.

COMPLAINING KILLS HAPPINESS

We have become a nation and a world of complainers. We hear it every day from those we work with, on the news and on television programs we listen to, and from those we live with. It is almost safe to say that most people even engage in complaining most if not all days of the week. The problem with habitual complaining is that it convinces you that all the goodness in the world is absent or lost. People who complain trap themselves in a reality that constantly gives them more to complain about. The old adage that says you *choose* whether to see the glass as half empty or half full is true. Even in identical circumstances some people will always see it as bad, and others will always view it as good.

A negative outlook is really just a habit – a habit that has the power to change the course of your life. You actively *choose* your outlook each and every day. The more you *choose* to be negative, even within your own mind, the more it becomes an ingrained habit and the harder it is to stop. Negativity becomes embedded in our minds subconsciously. It becomes so much a part of our lives that we don't even realize we're doing it. The sad part is that it affects everyone around us, from our coworkers to those we love, and we even pass on

this bad attitude and outlook to our children, creating another generation of unhappy and disappointed people.

We each live within a particular *comfort zone*, even if it's a bad one. Sometimes it's easier to stay in a familiar situation than to take a risk, even if that risk will improve your life. It's that old fear that while you have something right now that's not what you want, you still don't want to let it go and bet that you will have something better later. This can last for years for some people because after a while the attitude becomes ingrained and a part of the personality.

You can have a happy, satisfied life and you can choose it for yourself. You don't have to wait for some event to happen – like a raise at work or your children getting older or even winning the lottery! You simply have to train your mind to view your circumstances and opportunities in a different way. Part of this transformation is understanding that no one else can make you happy. Happiness is a choice and it's your choice. This means you must stop seeking external cures for your life and look inward.

"The difference between great people and everyone else is that great people create their lives actively, while everyone else is created by their lives, passively waiting to see where life takes them next. The difference between the two is the difference between living fully and just existing."

–MICHAEL E. GERBER
AUTHOR

Almost everywhere you turn these days you hear people say that their lot in life is not their fault. They had a hard childhood, were victims of some sort, or have no control over what happens. The truth is that there are circumstances that you don't – and won't ever – control. While you didn't necessarily choose those circumstances, you absolutely choose how you respond to them as a person and as a family. When you start playing the role of victim you become powerless. You hand the power to control your life over to others and then you feel forced to just take what comes. You can choose at any time to retake that power and change your life for the better, but you also have to take responsibility for yourself.

The idea of personal responsibility is completely opposite to the idea that nothing is your fault. Power in your life comes from knowing that whatever happens is your responsibility. It is this idea that keeps many people in their victimized complaining role. Honestly, it is so much easier to be a victim and sit around and complain than to get off the couch and take the steps necessary to change.

Here is a simple place to start. Read this affirmation twice a day out loud, once in the morning to start your day and once in the evening to end your day.

Life Affirmation
- I am responsible for my life.
- I am responsible for my feelings.
- I am responsible for my personal growth.
- I am responsible for every result I get.

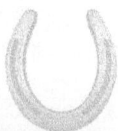

Change is scary. Failure is a possibility. Yet in order to be happy you must confront your fears and strive for the life you really want.

Many people tell stories about struggling for years in a situation before being almost forced to choose change. For us it was not years or even that we necessarily struggled. It was almost like we woke up one morning and took a hard look at where we were and where we wanted to go.

What we were doing was not going to get us what we wanted or more importantly where we needed to go. Times where changing in the cattle industry and if we did not figure something out we were going to be left behind. Even more important to us was the fact that if we did not make some changes our daughters would be left behind.

One of the hardest decisions that we had to face as a couple was that the lifestyle we loved could not ensure our financial future. In order to secure the financial future of our family, a huge part of the family business had to be let go of!

This was not easy; it was very scary. Buying and selling cattle was the way Jimmy had earned the bulk of his money since he purchased his first yearlings at the age of fourteen from a local auction market in Drayton Valley.

We knew what had to be done. The next step was to tell Jimmy's parents. Lori says that looking back, this was one of her proudest moment as Jimmy's wife. You see, once the decision was made, Jimmy faced it head on, knowing it was not going to be a popular one. Jimmy knew that things had to change – the decision was made, so let's move forward. That was exactly what happened.

Lori can still recall the scene from her kitchen window as a son broke the news to a father. The body language between the two men told the story; she did not have to hear the words exchanged between father and son.

Life changed that day and would never be the same, but that is what happens every day. No two days are exactly the same no matter how much we wish they could be.

It was a heart-wrenching time for the family; many words were exchanged in anger and fear. We were at a very bad place there for a while, but both of us knew that a price has to be paid for everything good in one's life.

Looking back now we can say that "as a couple we had drifted apart as more focus was required to keep what we had. The hard decisions we made then were the best ones we have ever made. We know that we are on a much better path for us as a couple, for our daughters and even for our extended family."

Change doesn't have to come from some challenging event, although it often does. It can also come because you are just very apathetic about your life. It's become a humdrum rut of existence as each day runs into the next. It's okay to feel bored with life, as it is an indicator that you are not accomplishing what you want. You may find yourself picking arguments with those around you and just being dissatisfied even if you can't pinpoint the problem. Simply accepting these emotions and doing nothing to change them can be dangerous as they may eventually build to a breaking point.

OVER-CONNECTED AND OVER-SCHEDULED

Do you ever wonder what it was like not to be connected 24/7? It's hard to believe but the electronic revolution has mostly occurred over the past ten to fifteen years. While these changes have brought some positive aspects to the way we live, they have also invaded every minute of every day for some people. One of the biggest aspects of finding happiness in your own life is the understanding that we all need some peace. This means time away from phones, computers, video games, and television. We need time to think about what we want as people and as a family unit. What is really important is making sure those important things get some attention.

We have noted before that some people seem to have so much more of everything than others. But think about this: everyone gets exactly the same amount of time – no more, no less. That amount is 1,440 minutes a day, 10,080 minutes a week, or 168 hours a week.

There are people entering adulthood today who have never known a world that wasn't always in chaos with no time to themselves. In fact, they don't know what to do with silence when it happens! It is very important when you think about changing your life that you find some type of sanctuary to get away from the noise of life. This might be a little cabin in the woods, a park in your neighborhood, or a seat at your own kitchen table (phones and TVs off!) – anywhere you can be alone with your thoughts and take an objective look at your life. Even as you are going through changes, it's always good to set aside a short time each day to clear your mind. Some people meditate, some pray, some just relax and breathe deeply.

Whatever method works for you, injecting an island of peace in your life is enough to give you some clarity about what you really want.

Of course, one of the biggest obstacles to finding peace is our overscheduled lifestyles. This is especially true for families. Not only do you have your own schedule to contend with as well as your spouse's, but you also have children who have piano lessons, hockey practice, or perhaps karate class. You may feel that you don't have a second to spare in the course of daily life – but this too is a *choice*. You have to give yourself permission to say no. If you never make time in your life for anything new or different, then you will continue to live your current life becoming more and more frustrated over time.

We often feel as if we must strive to do everything – give time to our community, our church, our children's school; but time is our most precious commodity and we don't realize we are giving it all away for things that aren't helping us be happy. You must *choose*. Taking responsibility for how you feel is more important than saying *"yes"* to everything so people will think you are a good person.

Thanks to one of our very special mentors, we have added this phrase to our vocabulary:

"Love to, can't now!"

GIVE IT A TRY!

Have you ever found yourself distorting reality to justify what you do? It's OK – we all tend to do that now and again. We overemphasize the importance of certain events so we don't feel like we are wasting our time on things that are insignificant – even though they are. It's much like someone who has a chronic negative outlook and who overemphasizes a particular event or news story to justify their continued stream of complaints. Both are distortions of reality. When you only focus on one tiny part of your life experience and fail to appreciate all the wonder and value of a better life experience, you are cheating yourself. If the negative or overscheduled "perspective" is supported and reinforced over time, it will become your habitual way of seeing the world. You will continue to rush through each day becoming more frazzled and allowing those important areas of your life to suffer.

Another simple trick we use to handle those times the sky seems to be falling is to think of one small thing you are *grateful for*. The power of that one small thing will surprise you with a smile on your face. Keep going until you forget why you felt the sky was falling.

The one thing that works for us is to hold our "gratitude rock." Our youngest daughter is a girl who can pick rocks all day – who sees and finds the beauty in the most "ordinary rock." So after hearing the story in "The Secret," we asked her to pick us each a rock which we carry with us every day. All we have to do is feel that rock in our hand and we have a reason to be grateful. Because we asked her to pick us a rock that first time, she now gives us rocks on a regular basis – she even gave one to her big sister the day she rode her new horse at their first rodeo together.

THE LAW OF ATTRACTION

If you've picked up a book, magazine, or searched the Internet recently, you've seen something written about *The Law of Attraction*. *The Law of Attraction* stipulates that we attract all the events in our lives. The majority of articles and teachings today talk about attracting success, money, and vitality through positive thinking. The flip side to this law is you also attract negatives into your life through *gloom-and-doom* thinking. If you focus on the fact that you have little money, bad health, or poor relationships, T*he Law of Attraction* responds by giving you more of what you are focusing on. This law isn't some guru's ploy to make money; it has been scientifically proven. So, why then do so many people choose negative thoughts and struggle through life?

One reason is a lack of patience. We want what we want, and we want it right now! Things take time to manifest in your life and when they don't occur instantly, many people go right back to their negative way of thinking. Those who truly understand the power of this law don't act this way. They understand that *The Law of Attraction* takes time to manifest in one's life. You wouldn't plant a garden and expect to have watermelons in a week. You must have faith and continue to work toward your goals. We often tell people that *The Law of Attraction* is like having blinders removed from your eyes: you will suddenly see help and opportunities that have always been there but which you weren't ready to see. It is much like going to a car lot and trading in your white car for a bright blue one. You buy the car thinking how unique it is, yet the minute you drive off the lot you suddenly see bright blue cars everywhere!

Does this mean they weren't there before? No. But you had a white car before and didn't notice the blues ones. It is much the same way when you change certain areas of your life.

"Great things take time to manifest."

We have found that by choosing fewer activities and by allowing time in our life for other things, there seem to be possibilities around every corner we turn. You can't expect that change will be dumped on you and somehow work out. You must make time and make room in your life, then take the steps toward your goals. If you sit on the couch and expect change to show up at your front door, you will be very disappointed. The whole idea is to start believing your life can change because without that belief it will never happen.

"Great things take time to manifest."

We wholeheartedly encourage each of you to give it a *whirl*. Just remember this is not something to *TRY;* you have to jump in with both feet and have some patience. After all, Rome was not built in a day!

This reminds us of a story we once read about a New York Times bestselling fiction author, Jodi Thomas. The story talks about the struggles Jodi had trying to get her first book published. Jodi was a schoolteacher by day and worked late into the night when her boys were small to finish that first book. Then she sent it out to every major publisher she could find in New York – and it came back with rejections almost just as fast. She was defeated and

losing hope. One day when she'd gotten a particularly nasty rejection letter she went to the local cemetery to sit and console herself. She often would go to a particular spot where benches surrounded a large stone bowl of fruit. As she sat and cried, she looked down at the stone beneath her feet and saw the word 'perseverance.' She walked all the way around the bowl of fruit, reading the words on each stone. It said, "Triumph Comes Through Perseverance." She resolved to try again and the very next publisher bought the book. She recently published her 29th novel.

This is proof that no one can believe for you. You must believe in yourself and your ability to make things happen before change will occur.

THE PIT OF DESPAIR

We admit that there have been times we've been in the pit of despair. There will always be circumstances and events that can really discourage you. When in the throes of one of life's challenges, it can be almost impossible to see the light of day. You may be in one of those places right now where it feels like your marriage and relationships are falling apart, like your children are becoming people you don't know, and the idea you had about where you'd be in life by now seems like some sort of sick fantasy.

Every person has these crises of faith on occasion, but only you can believe in you. Climbing out of where you are and getting to where you want to be takes much less effort than you think it will right now. Our perceptions become *warped* and it feels as if we are walking along an endless hallway to nowhere.

But you are making progress: if you choose to have a positive attitude and believe that your life will improve, then it will. You will see the actions and steps to take and take them.

> *"Faith is taking the first step even when you don't see the whole staircase."*
>
> –MARTIN LUTHER KING, JR.
> CLERGYMAN/ACTIVIST
> RALPH WALDO EMERSON
> POET/ESSAYIST

Life is simply a matter of *choice*. We get what we *choose*. Our life today is the direct result of the choices we made yesterday, and so will our life in the future be the result of the choices we make today. Everyone has the power of choice. Some just don't realize they have it or they choose not to use it.

Most people are only willing to change temporarily but not permanently. Permanent change requires commitment and discipline, but before discipline we need to have a clear objective. You must understand specifically what you want in order to move toward that goal.

It all starts with a clear understanding and a positive attitude, followed by actions, which influence our habits. These habits provide the discipline to sustain our continued commitment to reach our goals.

Change is never a question of *"can we do it?"* but it is actually a question of *"will we do it?"*

What about you?

Are you a DOER?

"Unless you try to do something beyond what you have already mastered, you will never grow."

—RALPH WALDO EMERSON
1803-1882, POET AND ESSAYIST

TWO

A THINKING PROBLEM

2% THINK

3% THINK THEY THINK

95% WOULD RATHER DIE THAN THINK

—DR KEN MCFARLAND
AUTHOR/SPEAKER

CHAPTER 2

The problem with stumbling through life is that we do so unconsciously, repeating what we learned or heard when we were young rather than consciously choosing where we want to go. *Awareness* of how you are living today versus how you really want to live is the first step to getting to a better, happier life.

At first glance it may seem that everyone stumbles through life getting by, and to a point that is true. But what's wrong with that? If everyone is dealing with life in the same way, then we're all in the same boat, right? Wrong. Very few people stop and think how much power they actually have to control their lives and *choose* their destiny. If you could, would you rather live a happy, joyful, prosperous life, or a stress, worried, and fearful one? That is a no brainer, right?

The choice is YOURS!   The choice is YOURS!

You can *choose* how you live and how you handle the challenges that arise in your life. While it may seem that the issues are all external, in reality they are all internal. If you are fed up and frustrated, it isn't your circumstances that are getting the best of you – it's your thought process.

The environments from which most self-made millionaires come was a surprise to us at the start of this journey. What they had to overcome to create what they have was a huge shock to us. Most of them say the first thing they had to get right was their THINKING. They had to start on the inside before they could create their outside world. Then they all learned to look for the circumstances they wanted; if they could not find those circumstances, they MADE them.

The mind is a powerful tool yet few people ever consciously consider what creates our thought patterns, feelings, and actions, and therefore what is responsible for the results we experience. Most of us stumble through life on autopilot, repeating the *beliefs*, *ideas* and *actions* that we have seen and experienced – the result of which is a rerun of our parents' or grandparents' lives. How many times have you wondered if you were turning into your mother or father when some phrase or idea slips from your mouth? That's because it is unconscious and affects your attitude every day.

ENVIRONMENT is more important than HEREDITY

When we think of *attitude*, positive thinking or having a bright and cheery attitude is what first comes to mind. While that is an important part of attitude, it is only a part of the truth. Attitude is a combination of your *thoughts, feelings,* and *actions* – not one of the three, but all of them working together. These thoughts, feelings, and actions are a product of our conditioned behavior, which includes how we were raised, education we were given, and the people who have influenced our lives. We are all a product of our individual experiences and thus each of us has a *unique* outlook and perspective on life. In order to understand how these ideas and actions have made us who we see in the mirror each morning, it is important to understand how we come to learn them in the first place.

We need to be made AWARE of how our thoughts, feelings, and actions come to LIFE.

Everything we know, we have learned in four specific stages.

The four stages are:
1. Unconscious Incompetence
2. Conscious Incompetence
3. Conscious Competence
4. Unconscious Competence

A great example of this learning process is how a baby learns to walk, and even more importantly, the stages of growth the baby goes through.

A baby follows his instinct to explore by first learning to crawl (unconscious incompetence). His DESIRE to explore develops his need to walk, so by holding firm to furniture he practices (conscious incompetence). The baby knows it's possible to walk; he's seen it done, and with determination and focus he keeps at it. The baby's walking improves; as long as he concentrates he can take a few short steps (conscious competence). When the walking moves to running and he is not thinking about each step, he is a master (unconscious competence). Once a process is learned, the mind moves it into the subconscious and it becomes a part of us that we no longer think about.

This same process is at work for each and everything we do without "thinking."

What we have learned is that in order to teach things which have moved to our subconscious, we MUST go back to conscious competence – for that is where we know the steps and can in turn teach them to others.

The goal of understanding this process is to realize why we do so many things in our lives that seem *unconscious*. It was not always that way, but because we are now on autopilot we have STOPPED THINKING. We keep following the same actions, which can only bring us the same results.

INSANITY
*"Doing the same thing each day
and expecting a different result."*

This is true of our careers, relationships, and how we raise our children. In order to change these ingrained habits, you must understand how the human mind works. As human beings, we think in pictures. If I told you to think of your car, your home, or your family, instantly pictures of these things flash on the screen of your mind. If I ask you to think of your mind, you might get a picture of your brain, but your brain is not your mind anymore than your fingernail is. The mind is much more than a particular group of cells inside your skull. One of the hardest things to understand is how the mind works until you have a picture of it. The most widely used illustration is the stick person developed in the 1930s by Dr. Thurman Fleet in San Antonio, Texas, and made popular by Bob Proctor from *The Secret*.

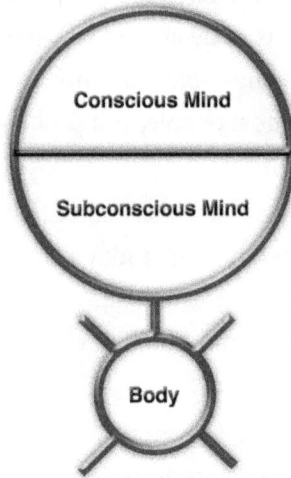

CONSCIOUS MIND

The top circle represents the mind or thoughts and the bottom circle represents your body or action. The mind is divided into the conscious and the subconscious. The conscious mind is where you receive all the input and experiences from your world. As you are faced with new events and ideas, your conscious mind has the ability to *accept or reject* any idea you choose. When thoughts come to you from your environment, the conscious mind is the filter which allows you to choose only those ideas and events you want to be emotionally involved with. The conscious mind is also where you create the dreams and *goals* that you want for your life as well.

It is estimated that today each person is bombarded and experiences tens of thousands of images per day. Of these images we can effectively capture or process about 1,000 on a conscious level. The information age has made our lives easier

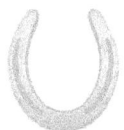

and more efficient with technology, but the price we pay is that there never seems to be any down time for our minds. We are constantly choosing what our mind will process and be exposed to, but like most people, you probably don't realize you have a *CHOICE!*

You MUST make a conscious choice to move your thoughts to the POSITIVE, because in today's world the NEGATIVE message is what makes the headlines. If you are constantly seeing negative images and hanging out with negative people, that is what you will become.

To think, feel, and act more positive, we MUST guard our subconscious with our conscious mind by being watchful of what ideas we get emotionally involved with and what images we are repeatedly viewing.

We are very LUCKY to have a ray of SUNSHINE in our home. Our oldest daughter has a bubbly personality that is infectious. Only now do we see the irony in our nickname for her: SUNSHINE. Her focus is always on the positive in any situation. Her weekly spelling test is a wonderful example. Monday she gets her list and she starts learning the words. She never talks about how many she gets wrong; her focus is on the number she gets right. She never questions whether she will get a perfect mark come Friday. Being around such people makes you focus on the POSITIVE in all situations and results in having a POSITVE nature.

So if we could give you each a piece of advice it would be: find that ray of sunshine and consciously choose to face towards it!

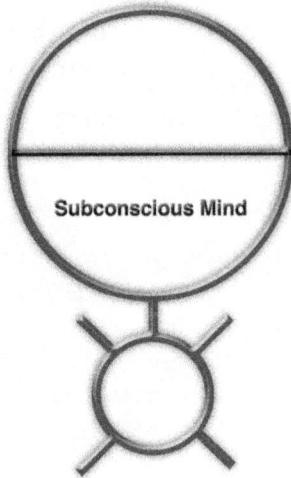

SUBCONSCIOUS MIND

This is the *"emotional mind"* or *"feeling mind."* The ancient Greeks called it *"The heart of hearts."* The subconscious mind only has one answer to all commands it receives from the conscious mind, and that answer is *"YES!"*

The subconscious mind has *"NO"* ability to *accept* or *reject* thoughts. This is why it is important to monitor thoughts and ideas as we receive them into our conscious mind. If we worry about something happening then the subconscious will move us in the direction of having exactly what we were worrying about.

Likewise, if we create a positive idea of how we want events to go or how we want to handle the unfortunate things that happen in our lives, then the subconscious mind can and will manifest that positive result.

Worrying and focusing on what you don't want takes just as much energy and time, if not more, than focusing on what you do want. The BEST part of this is that it WORKS! You will always attract more of the same energy you are in *harmony* with; if that energy is negative, then that's what you will receive.

*"When you focus on what's WRONG,
you get more of what's WRONG.*

*Conversely, when you focus on what's RIGHT,
you get more of what's RIGHT."*

—GINA MOLLICONE-LONG
AUTHOR

The encouraging message from understanding how the subconscious mind works is that we can monitor our conscious mind, and more importantly, use auto-suggestion to increase our positive results. We create the thoughts and ideas we want, and through repetition of these thoughts they become real in our lives.

*"A human being always acts, feels, and performs
in accordance with what he imagines to be true
about himself and his environment. This is a basic
and fundamental law of the mind.
It is the way we were built."*

—MAXWELL MALTZ, M.D.
AUTHOR

It's been said that you can never outperform your self-image. What do you think of yourself? Why not imagine yourself *wealthy, healthy,* and *happy*?

Some good questions to ask yourself to give you an idea of what your self-image is right now are:

- Would you like to be working for or with a *person* like you?
- Would you strike up a conversation with someone who has your attitude?
- Would you like to come home to a spouse like you?
- Would you like to have a parent like you?
- Would you like to have a friend like you?

If your self-image is that you are an unattractive, boring, terrible person, would you want to have anything to do with you? You must start mentally being the person you want to become because you will only do or have the things you want if you first start being that person. Many people have it backwards. These people often say: "If I only had an understanding wife, then I would do the things required and I would be a good husband. " What they should think is: "I am a good husband, therefore I do what's required in a relationship and as result we have a good marriage."

Start from the inside and work out!

When we get emotionally involved with a dream or goal and it enters the subconscious, the mind *"locks in"* to that emotion. Failure then becomes negative feedback and allows you to make a conscious correction and get back on course. This is comforting because the minute that you have your goal locked in on the subconscious level you cannot miss your target – if you stay in action always moving forward and don't adjust your setting by becoming complacent.

THE BODY

The body is the physical form and machine that is created and recreated daily by our dominant thoughts and actions. The body carries out actions based on directions from the conscious and subconscious mind. It is the evidence of what is held in the mind.

Lori has participated in the sport of curling for many years and uses this method to help her accomplish her goals on the ice.

Many sports teams use the power of their minds to enhance their performance on the field or on the ice. In my sport, I visualize my movements as I release the curling stone toward the target. I see my teammates helping guide the stone and visualize the shot being made just as the skip called it. Since the subconscious mind cannot tell the difference between real and imagined, this mental

workout is as important as physical practice because when it comes time to perform, the mind directs your actions. When I use this method, most often the result is very positive. This same technique is used by world-class basketball players, golfers, and top-level athletes from many sports. It makes sense that if it works so well in the sports arena, it will work equally well in other areas of our life.

When we change the thoughts to which we give the most focus and energy and repeat these thoughts until they become ideas, we alter the ideas that are impressed upon our subconscious mind, which again changes how we *feel, act,* and *respond.*

"Dream lofty DREAMS,
and as you dream, so shall you become.

Your VISION is the promise of
what you shall one day be.

Your IDEAL is the prophecy
of what shall at last unveil."

–JAMES ALLEN
AUTHOR

DECISION MAKING

Decision Making is an ART, which like
learning to walk has to be taught.

The problem is we are never taught how to make decisions in school. Most people today, when faced with making a decision, simply ask the people around them: "What do you think?" The fact is that most people don't consciously think. We have opinions based on emotion, guesswork, and often fear – but we don't actively and consciously consider a situation before we offer an opinion on it or make a decision about the best course of action.

The reason so few of us actively think is that it is much easier to let our subconscious take over. To actively consider an event or course of action, you must push away the other images that are bombarding your conscious mind and focus. Henry Ford put it best when he said, *"Thinking is hard work, that's why so few engage in it."* He's right. It is very hard work to change your habits and feelings and force yourself to consider alternative possibilities before making a decision.

Instead, we listen to *"conventional wisdom," to* what others say, to what we read in the newspaper or see on TV or in the latest BLOG. Everyone has an opinion, and as Napoleon Hill points out in *Think & Grow Rich*, "Opinions are the cheapest commodities on earth." Nonetheless, it is amazing how strong people's opinions can be on subjects that they have little knowledge or experience in.

To start charting your own flight plan you MUST turn the following KEY of change. You MUST do your own research and make up your own MIND. Stop blindly following *"conventional wisdom,"* and more importantly, stop blindly accepting *"conventional wisdom."* We must learn to chart our own path.

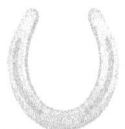

The Kennedy Family is a wonderful example:

Joseph P. Kennedy instilled in his sons and daughters a "critical mind."

A critical mind is one that does not blindly accept what is generally considered fact but rather uses its own ability, willingness, and obligation to do one's own research and make one's own decisions.

The success of Joe Kennedy and the accomplishments of his family can be attributed to the development of a "CRITICAL MIND.."

Ask yourself what would have happened if John F. Kennedy had listened and let other convince him that it was a waste of time to try going to the moon.

Following or blindly accepting *"Conventional Wisdom"* not only limits you to your own experience, but to the equally limited experience and opinions of others. For example, you may look at your bank account and let that dictate your opportunities for financial growth. When an opportunity comes along that excites you, and you ask others what they think about it, they will often respond negatively based on what they have heard or the opinions they have gathered – not on the facts. This is true in all areas of life. How often have you met those that let their past relationships dictate their belief in new relationships? When a new relationship comes along, how often do these same people ask others for advice only to be reminded of their own past failures? This is not active thinking or decision making.

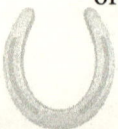

Most people think biographically
– we LIVE what our past was.

With the fast-pace world we live in people do not allow themselves time to think, thus they have lost the skill of knowing how to think; instead, we allow ourselves to be taught *what* to think, but not *how* to think. We all need to go back to grade one and remember how we were taught to do addition. Instead of memorizing the answers to a math problem, the teacher put groups of objects in front of us and showed us how to calculate it for ourselves. Human beings have been given intellectual faculties which allow us to think and create whatever we want; the problem is we do not use them often enough or use them properly. The faculties of *Reasoning, Intuition, Perception, Will, Imagination,* and *Memory* need to be exercised just like muscles. We can train ourselves to take control of how we think, feel, and act, thus controlling the results we get. Most people are actually using the intellectual faculties to their disadvantage. For example, memories of failure which are visited repeatedly in the mind can convince even the most capable person that they are doomed to fail.

We see this in many of life's pages: A cowboy who is an expert roper misses a few and starts losing faith in himself, instead of replaying the seven-second run that won him the gold buckle he so proudly wears. When he revisits these times they will bring back the "vibration" of success. A relationship starts going bad and the couple focuses on the problems instead of remembering all the good things and feelings which brought them together. A businessperson goes bankrupt and instead of getting up and

starting again, loses himself to the fresher memories of failure and deserts entrepreneurship completely, instead of learning from the temporary setbacks and viewing them as just that – temporary.

THE COMPARISON PARADOX

One of the most common beliefs is that "MONEY" is the source of all "EVIL." The money is not evil, only the actions that can be paid for with it. We have come to the understanding that money, like everything else, just "is." It only makes you more of what you already are; it doesn't change you. If you are a good person, it will make you a great person; if you are a bad person, more money will probably make you a terrible person. There are many examples of good people with a great deal of money giving back – Bill Gates and Warren Buffet, to mention a couple. Therefore, as a friend of ours once said, *"If you consider yourself a good person – get rich!"* In other words, if you want to help others, help yourself first. You cannot give what you do not have. So what is holding you back? Like many people you probably suffer from what is known as the "comparison paradox."

> ### *Money is like the ultimate servant.*
> ### *The more you earn, the more you can help others.*

Most of us learned very early in life to compare ourselves to others. We carry around the idea that we are *"average,"* meaning we are within a range of lifestyle that is comfortable and comparable to our friends, neighbors, parents, and siblings.

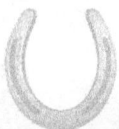

What it really means is that we are limiting ourselves through comparison to others. We create within our own minds an idea of what is *"probable"* rather than *"possible."* Thus when we try to set goals, we start out by deciding what we can realistically get and then take steps to achieve that limited goal. A good example would be to look at income statements of what you earned last year, then stretch it a little to what you think you can earn and set your goal there. This goal may only be 5-20 % higher than last year. The problem isn't that you can't meet that goal – you can. The problem is that the goal is too limited to begin with, and instead of contemplating what you really want, you force yourself into a series of very small steps to reach what you think you can achieve.

This same idea is also at work in our relationships. You may be in a roomful of people, some very attractive and others more average. If you consider yourself *average,* you will only approach those you think are within your ability to attract and therefore you may pass by a wonderful person who is your soul mate.

Jimmy talks about how this would have been true for him had he not taken a risk and gone for what he wanted.

To not go after something or someone that you think is unachievable is where most make their biggest mistake. It is when you go after what many may see as the unachievable that the biggest strides in life are made and are usually made the fastest.

Jimmy says: I knew I was not the hottest guy out there as far as attracting Lori. There were others who I knew had gone there and thought they knew her. What I now realize is they just didn't take the risk. They told me I did not stand a chance – if I had

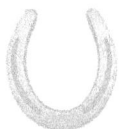

listened to them and sold myself short I would have missed out. I knew what I had to offer – I was living from the inside out. If I was to stand a chance I had to make sure she got to know who I really was, and I had to let her know that I was interested in all of her. Lori's beauty was what most of the other guys saw and were interested in – but it was Lori's confidence that made me risk.

They were scared to take a risk and get shot down – I knew she was what I wanted so I took a risk. If I would have been scared and sold myself short I would have not risked getting shot down and missed out on my soul mate.

Let me tell you: if you are scared to take a big step because you might fail, you can only achieve small outcomes in life and you will be settling for second best.

Not only is the comparison paradox active in our personal lives, it is frequently seen in the business arena as well.

Let's say you work in a large corporation, and each year you must budget for the next year's sales. Normally you might argue for a 10% increase, knowing the board/owners would ask for 30%. Thus the "goal" is set at 20%. This is a prognosis rather than a goal. Instead of striving to be number one in the market, you only strive to improve upon last year's performance and limit your performance in advance to no more than a 20% increase at best. What if you aimed for the top, even if it meant doubling your sales? The truth is you may never know if you limit your potential achievements before even trying.

To be our best at anything in life you have to set #1 type GOALS!

When we set #1 type goals we move to a higher achievement...

Live the dream...

And enjoy success on a totally new level.

The problem with the comparison paradox is that it allows us to believe that we are setting goals and making progress – a good thing in most people's minds. In reality, it limits us to a predetermined outcome and cheats us of our true potential.

Please do not permit what is happening around you to determine what you think.

Do not become a toy for outside forces.

Reclaim you MIND!

Let it help you get what you want!

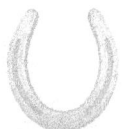

THREE

HAPPINESS IS A CHOICE

"Be HAPPY with what you have while pursuing what you WANT.

The KEY to happiness is not MORE."

—JIM ROHN
AUTHOR/ENTREPRENEUR/SPEAKER

CHAPTER 3

Happiness, what is it to you? Not the same thing it was when you were a child or a teenager! To most, the definition of happiness is: Do we have what we WANT? As time goes by what we want from life changes, transforming what HAPPINESS is to us. The key is not to associate HAPPINESS with the pursuit of what we WANT. When we associate the two together the result is the feeling that the quest for happiness is an illusion which we will never fully achieve. As William Dempster Hoard once said, *"Happiness doesn't depend on what we have, but it does depend on how we feel towards what we have. We can be happy with a little and miserable with much."* Happiness is a state of MIND, much like a positive attitude, and should not be defined by our WANTS! When we realize that happiness and wants should not be grouped together we will be given the OK to change. We can *choose* to be happy in any situation knowing that happiness is not a singular destination but part of a journey, and that our WANTS are just stops along the journey to our destiny. There is no need to wait for *'someday'* or to put it off. How long you have been in a situation or how chaotic your

life is right now makes no difference. You can simply make the *CHOICE* to be *HAPPY*!

Allowing yourself to be *HAPPY* in any situation is not going to be easy. You may think you have tried to change in the past, but nothing worked. Why? One of the reasons may have been that you kept breaking the commitments you made to yourself and then found excuses why it wasn't your fault. If this sounds at all familiar, it may be because you see yourself as a victim of your circumstances and feel like you don't have a *choice*. In order to change your life you must understand that you do have a *choice,* and with this comes a strong sense of personal accountability.

In today's world most workplaces use accountability as a form of assigning BLAME; that is the main reason people resist being accountable. The resistance comes from FEAR, first the fear of being blamed when something goes WRONG, and second the fear of FAILURE. No one wants to look bad, make mistakes, or feel incompetent. To avoid feeling that way, we simply don't challenge ourselves. Finally, we avoid accountability for fear of success.

What we need to know is that accountability simply means doing what you say you're going to do. It's simple, but not easy. If it were, people wouldn't so often fail to keep their commitments and that's unfortunate, because accountability can totally transform your life. It makes everything possible.

If we increase accountability, we will accomplish more, we'll be held to a higher standard of performance, and we'll maintain excellence. It is much easier to dream of success than to actually achieve it.

While sitting around at Christmas and New Years there always tends to be talk of resolutions. As a friend talked of her need to look for a new job because she wasn't really satisfied with the one she had, she said she should make this a goal for herself for the upcoming year. The sad thing was that in her very next breath she went on to say that she doesn't set goals because she never succeeds in achieving them. We now know that she did not want to set a goal as we sat there listening because she would have to be accountable for it. If she didn't set a goal or if she only made a commitment to herself, she could then make excuses when the goal was not attained.

We would just like to say: Set goals and share them with everyone; put yourself out there. The only thing you risk is that things stay exactly as they are.

> *"It is not that we can't do great things,*
> *It's just that we won't attempt to do great things."*

> –PAUL ORBERSON
> AUTHOR

STEPS TO ACHIEVE
PERSONAL ACCOUTABLITY

REJECT THE VICTIM SYNDROME

> *"No snowflake in an avalanche ever feels responsible."*

> –VOLTAIRE
> PHILOSOPHER

What is the VICTIM SYNDROME?

It is the situation that arises when things happen to you and you don't feel you have a *choice* in the matter which sets up a victim mentality. Simply stated, when faced with a situation, you ignore, deny, blame, rationalize, resist, and ultimately hide. The unsettling truth is people usually *choose* to be victims. It is a *MINDSET*.

This has become such a common occurrence and is so prevalent that many individuals don't even realize they are doing it. People who smoke and drink too much would, for example, often rationalize their behavior by blaming stress, their boss at work, being a single parent, or financial difficulty.

Our mindset changed one spring day in a rodeo arena. At the time we had no idea this was the day we would look back on as the start of our journey.

We watched as the association rationalized and blamed Jimmy for the accident. Referring to the steps described above, they were using rationalization and blame to justify their actions. The hard truth of it is they had been ignoring a situation that had been present for many years, one that was just laying in wait for its chance to EXPLODE!

The association, along with many of the contestants who had rodeoed with Jimmy for years, moved through the steps of denial, blame, rationalization, and resistance through the many weeks and months of our battle with them.

As we moved past this very hard time we were lucky because we learned to take actions that moved us away from allowing ourselves to be victims. For the association and the contestants

involved, the pattern has seemingly not changed – reactive action is still the course rather than proactive action. The result is they are still complaining about the same things – nothing has changed – they are still playing that same VICTIM Syndrome!

Ignore, Deny, Blame, Rationalize, Resist, and ultimately Hide are still their course of ACTION today.

It is our HOPE that by sharing this with you each of you will realize that only YOU can change the pattern – you will have to be strong and never give up. But the one thing we can assure you of is there is a much better life on the other side!

Change your MINDSET – choose to stop being a VICTIM!

We want to take this opportunity to say how grateful and thankful we are to those who stood with us during this hard time. It made all the difference then, and it is something that we held close during this journey and will remain a part of each journey we take in the future. We love each of you and you will always hold a special place in our hearts!

These words are for you:

> *"People of character do the right thing, not because they think it will change the world but because they refuse to be changed by the world."*

> –MICHAEL JOSEPHSON
> RADIO COMMENTATOR

When you move from being a victim to being accountable, you realize that regardless of what has happened to you in the past, you can choose what you do next. Other people or outside circumstances do not control what you think or how you feel about yourself. Breaking free of the victim mindset allows you to move into action. In this way you regain power over a life that seems to be passing you by.

TAKE CONTROL OF YOUR LIFE

A "Crystal Clear" Picture

Now it is time for step number two: you must clarify what real success looks like to you. Define your purpose, vision, and goals. When Jim Carrey was a struggling actor in the mid-1980s and couldn't even pay the rent, he wrote himself a check in the amount of $10 million "for acting services rendered." Twenty years later he makes over $20 million per movie – now that's a vision! While your vision may be different, you must see it just as clearly, as if you already have it and can imagine yourself enjoying the fruits of your labor.

Once you have defined your purpose and refined your vision of success, put together a list of accountability goals that will take you there. But beware of one of the surprising pitfalls of accountability: perfectionism. Many people put off starting their journey until they know every single step along the way. That is a mistake. Your path will twist and turn and there is no way to know where those changes will lead as you work toward your goal. If you wait until you have perfected the journey, you

will never take the first step. Remember what John Updike said: *"Perfectionism is the enemy of creation."*

Progress before perfection – start with what you have. In the beginning it can be better to think less and do more.

> *This is a huge lesson and a hard one to learn.*
> *But know this – if you wait, your results will be*
> *trapped by reasons and those reasons will keep*
> *you trapped for LIFE!*

There are a few things that you MUST do to ensure your SUCCESS. The first is to write it down. Lori learned this firsthand from her years as a laboratory technologist: *"If it isn't written down, it did not happen."* We know that it is the one step that is most often forgotten when people set out on this kind of journey. The second thing to keep in mind is you MUST write your statements as if they have already happened.

> *"Whatever the MIND can CONCEIVE and*
> *BELIEVE it can ACHIEVE."*
>
> –NAPOLEON HILL
> AUTHOR

BE HONEST

Until you know all the areas of your life that need growth and are willing to be honest about them, you can't do anything differently. Sometimes a problem can look very big because you are stepping into a vast unknown to find solutions. But

when you look behind the curtain, you will see that the wizard is just a person and those solutions weren't nearly as hard or scary as you thought. So take an objective and unbiased look at where you really are.

The challenge is to attain a neutral frame of mind, marked by compassion, openness, and sincerity. Please don't judge your past actions or let resentment or guilt take over. Your best thinking brought you to this point—if you had known how to do any better, you would have done it. Your current reality is a starting point for learning and moving forward.

> *"Get over it because nothing will keep you more emotionally, physically and financially broke than constantly thinking about the past.*
>
> —PAUL ORBERSON
> AUTHOR

TAKE OWNERSHIP

Consider this: when you own something, you are much more likely to respect it. When was the last time you took a rental car through the car wash? Never? When you are working on a project with other people, assume 100% of the ownership in your own mind. Don't become a power-hungry dictator who takes all the credit, or a martyr who takes all the blame, or a sidestepper who takes none of the blame. Find a good balance of responsibilities while keeping in mind that at the end of the day, what needs to be done needs to be done. You can't wait for someone to come along and help or do it for you. You are responsible.

*"If you are not afraid to face the music,
someday you will lead the band."*

EMBRACE FORGIVENESS

Once you have recognized the reality of your circumstance and take ownership of the part you have played to get there, forgiveness is your way out – not an excuse to do something that doesn't work, but an opportunity to wipe the slate clean and give it another try. Forgiveness is not a substitute for corrective action, but a way to come to the action in a more creative, caring way. If a thought serves you, it is welcome to stay. If it paralyzes you, it has to go. Period.

"You may have a fresh start any moment you choose,

for this thing that we call FAILURE,

is not the falling down,

but the STAYING DOWN."

–MARY PICKFORD
ACTRESS/PRODUCER

SELF-EVALUATION

*Put "Conventional Wisdom" in its place
and develop a "Critical Mind."*

Awareness is the turning point. From here, you can start creating your new life. It's time to get rid of your automatic pilot syndrome which is *thinking, doing,* and/or *feeling* the same things repeatedly, and instead make deliberate, purposeful *choices.* You may feel that you have no control over your circumstances, and it's certainly true that you can't control other people. But what you can control is how you respond and react. Ask yourself: how might I have created, promoted, or allowed the situation I am in? If you are honest, you will see that you did play a role in your current situation, even if you merely sat back and let it happen.

A couple of years ago we were inspired by an interesting story we heard about a woman who suddenly became the owner of the business when her husband passed away. The woman's late husband had been running their business for many years and though she was aware of what they did, he made the day-to-day decisions. To all others around her, the woman was said to know little about the business, and upon his death, people expected she would sell it. When she announced that she would visit with the management team, they assumed it was to announce the sale. On the contrary, she asked to meet all managers separately.

She asked each one of them the same three questions: 1) What are you doing? 2) What works? 3) What doesn't? Then she empowered them to stop doing what doesn't work and do more of what was working or find new solutions to what didn't work. She came back week after week and rehearsed these questions with the management team and they started doing the same with their employees.

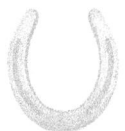

This simple method created an inspired organization. You can use this same method in your personal life as well. You could, for example, in a marriage or relationship ask yourself, *"How do we ignite and renew the excitement in our relationship? What are we doing, what's working and what isn't?"*

NEVER CEASE TO LEARN

> *"Today the single greatest source of wealth is between your ears."*
>
> —BRIAN TRACY
> AUTHOR

Seize the opportunity and let yourself be transformed. Think differently. If what you did in a previous situation didn't work out, the process of learning guarantees you will proceed differently next time. Leave your ego at the door. To be a master learner, you must believe that you know nothing. In this way, you are able to replace old paradigms and learn from your new coach or mentor. In order to learn, you need to have just enough self-esteem. Too little self-esteem and you don't think you can learn, too much and you don't think you need to learn.

Lori shares this story:

I remember a time during my career as a laboratory technologist that I was sent on a training course; it was a supervisor course. As they were not sending all the supervisors and I was neither the newest nor the most experienced, it was

hard to understand. Instead of seizing the opportunity I found myself trying to justify – why me. There were others who knew less than me and some who knew more – so I broke the rules about learning – I did not check my ego at the door and I certainly did not believe that I knew nothing. I did learn some very valuable things in the course but not nearly as much as I would today.

Today I would seize the opportunity because I have learned that the "teacher will appear when the student is ready," and even more importantly, "the teacher will appear even if the student does not realize she is ready." I now look at learning in a whole different light and I am excited each and every time I am given the opportunity to learn. More than anything else I am grateful for what my mentors have shared with me – their knowledge.

> "Never regard study as a duty, but as the enviable opportunity to learn to know the liberating influence of beauty in the realm of the spirit, for your own personal joy and to the profit of the community to which your later work belongs."
>
> —ALBERT EINSTEIN
> PHYSICIST

TAKE ACTION

To like your life – the sum of your actions – you have to like each action individually. Take small, manageable actions that take you beyond your *comfort zone* but don't paralyze you. Keep moving toward your goal. Reach out for help when you need it. If there's one certainty in life it's that things will not

go according to plan! Knowing this, you must also understand why you shouldn't wait for all to be perfect before acting. Act with what you have and make corrections along the way.

For example, we have a friend who talks about but never starts his own business. He has thought about it for a long time. He produces Excel spreadsheets; he plans and strategizes in detail while waiting for the timing to be "just right" but he never starts. Truth is, you will probably never have the exact right timing or the perfect economy – just start it or you will wind up like this friend and years slip past with no forward progress.

"Everyone who has ever taken a shower has had an idea. It's the person who gets out of the shower, dries off, and does something about it that makes a difference."

–NOLAN BUSHNELL
ENTREPRENEUR

Plan what you'll do when you get off course – as long as you remind yourself of your purpose, you will be able to recover from your mistakes.

Ultimately there is no end or limit to the rewards of a life lived with personal accountability, and anyone who longs for freedom should heed the message. When you commit to accountability, everything else falls into place. Your relationships become deeper, more honest, more fulfilling. Your career takes off. Your health improves. Accountability unleashes your creativity and expands your ability to love and be loved. The accountable person knows that anything is possible and is not afraid to get out there and achieve it.

PERSONAL RESPONSIBILITY

Often people use the words 'accountability' and 'responsibility' interchangeably but they are very different. Accountability is doing what you say you will do, but responsibility is understanding that no matter what the outcome, *the buck stops with you*. When we take responsibility, we admit we are the ones responsible for the *choices* we have made and continue to make. We, not other people or events, are responsible for the way we *think* and *feel*. It is our life, and we are in charge of it. We are free to enjoy it or disdain it. While we are not responsible for all that happens to us, we are responsible for how we *think, feel,* and *respond* to those circumstances.

Many people associate responsibility with duty and obligations, which, in turn, are thought of as burdens. But personal responsibility is not a burden, it is a gift. This becomes clear when we understand that personal responsibility is nothing but the freedom to create our own lives. Once we awaken to this fact, we are liberated and empowered. We shed the victim mentality and gain the power to transform ourselves.

Ask yourself "WHY" we:

Reject the roles of creativity, flexibility, and resiliency in order to play the role of victim?

Choose to be weak when we can be strong?

Choose to be sullen when we can be thrilled?

Let's get personal and talk about you for a moment. Are you perfectly happy with the way things are at this time, or do you wish things were better? Chances are you are neither perfectly happy nor completely unhappy, for most of us lie somewhere between both extremes.

If you wish to change, why not begin by recognizing that your present situation is not the result of your genes, parents, education, job, luck, timing, health, or environment. Rather, it is the *choices* you have made and the *actions* you have taken which have brought you to where you are today. Change your *choices* and *actions* and you will change the results that follow.

> *"Don't be afraid to give up the*
> *GOOD to go for the GREAT."*
>
> —KENNY ROGERS
> SINGER/ACTOR

Examine your life to learn the extent to which you are either already taking responsibility or evading it.

Do you ever say to yourself:

- Life is so unfair.
- I'm unlucky.
- No one wants to help me.
- It's not my fault that I'm the way I am.
- Life is an endless struggle; there are too many burdens to bear.
- Terrible things are always happening to me.

- Other people and events (spouse, friends, coworkers, boss, health, the weather, or the political situation) make me depressed (angry or frustrated).
- I feel overwhelmed and helpless.
- Some people get all the breaks; I'm just unfortunate.

This list is endless. Instead of taking personal responsibility and taking charge of your life, that kind of thinking is used to blame others or life for your own failures.

It's easy to shift the responsibility and blame others or events. But what good is that? All it does is keep us in our *comfort zone* and allow us or those we know to continue to echo negatively.

We cannot make any real progress until we admit to ourselves:

Only I can:

- Hold myself back.
- Stand in my own way.
- Help myself.
- Take personal responsibility.
- Transform myself from a victim of circumstances to a reasoning, decision-making, action-oriented person.
- Only I can take charge of my life.

One of the first *'people'* we greet each morning is our reflection in the mirror. For that reason we have to be accountable, answerable, and responsible for the life we are creating for ourselves. By accepting that responsibility, we

unleash great power and the ability to transform ourselves. Though it may be hard to accept the fact that no one limits your options but you, it is a necessary part of the process of change. The ability to grasp the power hidden inside is one that few people ever find.

If you want to make a few tiny steps, greet yourself each morning as you look into the mirror with the following words of *wisdom* offered to us by a very dear friend and mentor, Floyd Wickman.

It takes as much PAIN to SUCCEED as it does to FAIL!

My choice is to SUCCEED!

If anyone "CAN" – I "CAN"!

If it is to BE, It is up to ME!

Say this each and very time you find yourself stepping or slipping back in the Victim Syndrome. It sure has helped us stay on track and ever more importantly get back on track!

This emphasis on making the right choices and accepting personal responsibility is for your benefit only. That is, use these ideas to improve yourself, but not to judge others. You can never enter the *mind, heart,* and *body* of another, so you are unaware of the reasons for their failures. Not everyone is as ready as you are to change.

Happiness is a choice, just like misery is.

JIMMY & LORI GUNSCH

We all have the responsibility to make the right *choices* for ourselves but we can't make those choices for others. It is natural progression once you understand this principle to experience some frustration as you see coworkers, family members, and friends continue to exhibit negative or even destructive behavior. You must have patience. As they see your life change and improve, they will become aware of the areas they might change. It will be then that you will truly realize the widespread positive influence you have with everyone you come in contact.

In life you have many *choices*; one is to take 100% responsibility for whatever happens in your life, as well as in your business if you have one. There is no point in blaming *circumstances, environment,* and *conditions.* We know and now you are aware that playing the victim while blaming the economy of the country, your family background, or the politicians and society for your results won't get you anywhere.

It is not our responsibility to make others happy, any more than it is it theirs to make us happy. Each of us is responsible for our own happiness. As you move to this attitude, you have to remember to clearly state what you want in all situations, not what you think someone else would like to hear. Using this very clear and direct form of communication will create an environment where no one will feel "hurt."

We encourage you can make this decision: It is your responsibility to have a fulfilling life and to be happy, not your wife's or husband's or the government's or your parents.' Your employees and the financial performance of your business are also not to blame.

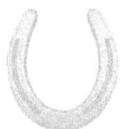

By being accountable and accepting responsibility for where you are in life will allow you to be open and move along the path to fulfillment at a rapid pace.

"Happiness is to be found along the way,
not at the end of the road for then the JOURNEY is
over and it is too LATE!

Today, this hour, this minute is the DAY, the hour,
the minute for each of us to sense the fact that LIFE is
GOOD, with all of its trials and troubles, and perhaps
more interesting because of THEM."

—ROBERT R
AUTHOR

FOUR

BEHIND DOOR NUMBER THREE

"Sometimes we stare so long at a door that is closing, That we see too late the one that is open."

—ALEXANDER GRAHAM BELL
INVENTOR

CHAPTER 4

We all have ideas at certain points in our lives of how things will be. This is good in some ways as it allows us to hope for the future. But life changes constantly and when we hold on to an ideal whose time has passed, it can actually interfere with enjoying our lives now. A great example is, if you hold onto a dress or suit for ten years hoping that you will fit into it again, you are cheating yourself of enjoying who you are now. It's as if you are longing for the person that once was instead of realizing all that you've learned and how far you have come.

In today's world the one thing that families often face is that they are always on the go somewhere. It is very important that we are not so focused on where we are going that we forget to enjoy the now. There is an old saying that the *days are long*, but the *years are short* and this is especially true when you have children. It is easy to focus on the trials and tribulations of each day rather than focusing on the moments of connection that fill your heart with joy.

In order to have the life you want, you must decide what that life looks like based on what is, not what you think it should have been. This means setting goals and priorities – as a person, couple, and family, even if that means letting go of a few things. There are those things we do as parents sometimes that we think we should – such as taking our children to music lessons or getting them involved is several sports. Yet you must balance that with the actual wants of the child and the goals of the family. Is it more important that your child attend every soccer game or spend time with a grandparent who will not be around forever? When you point out this type of choice, the answer seems obvious, but often we don't really think about it as a choice. We just continue in our routine assuming that activity equals quality.

In order to get a vague idea of what you want to accomplish as a family, you have to set very clear goals and then break those goals into doable steps. While this takes some time to outline, it will keep you moving forward toward your goals and allow you to see when you get distracted or fall off the intended path. Some find goal-setting a tedious process but it is powerful because it forces you to look at what you are doing and where you are going. Every path in life is a choice we have made; when we have clear goals those *choices* are much easier to make. We find crystal clear goals are very motivating. They make you push yourself, and without these really strong goals we tend to slack off and do what's easy rather than striving for more.

"If you don't design your own life plan, chances are you'll fall into someone else's plan.

And guess what they have planned for you?

Not MUCH!"

–Jim Rohn
Entrepreneur/Author/Speaker

Each of us must realize that the people in life who are succeeding at the highest level – no matter if they are an executive, rodeo athlete, or business owner – set goals. They make time in their busy schedules to set daily, weekly, monthly, and yearly goals, as well as long-term multiyear goals. If all the people at the top are doing this, do you not think it makes sense that you should be doing it too? You BET it does! Setting goals and writing them down gives you a distinct advantage. There is no way to maintain a long-term vision as well as short-term motivation without setting goals and writing them down. The last step is to track the goals that you have set.

By setting clear and well-defined goals, you can evaluate your progress and take pride in your accomplishments. You can confirm that you are making progress though it might seem at times that you are not moving much. The greatest benefit of written goals is that it allows you to look back and see how far you've come, how much you have grown.

JIMMY & LORI GUNSCH

"A good plan is like a road map:
it shows the final destination

and usually the best way to get there."

–H. STANLEY JUDD
AUTHOR

SETTING EFFECTIVE GOALS

If you have an idea for a business you want to try, or if you have an idea of what you want to accomplish with your family, you must focus those ideas. Until you have those ideas defined and organized, you won't have a clear direction. Define and organize them into a *"crystal clear picture."*

What we have discovered is that there are both good goals and less effective goals. We have learned that all good goals have a few things in common:

DEFINED

In order to be as effective as possible, your goals must be written in a way that is very clearly defined. Write what you WANT not what you do not WANT. The goal must be specific and something that you can attach to emotionally. This means that you must use words that describe your goals – paint that *"crystal-clear picture."* Instead of saying, *"I don't want to argue,"* you write, *"I see myself calmly handling all the events of my day."* It's like watching a movie that doesn't make sense; you can't really get involved as it is unclear what the point is, so be specific and clearly outline your goals.

- 71 -

TIMEFRAME

It's important that you put a timeframe on your goals, otherwise they remain merely wishes which you will never push yourself to achieve. You must pick a timeframe that is reasonable but at the same time challenges you. These self-imposed deadlines put pressure on you to accomplish your goals. Because you placed timeframes on your goals you will be able to determine if you are making progress. Without timeframes there's no way to measure your progress. For example, if you set a goal to run a marathon but you don't say what marathon or when, why would you get up and train each morning?

COMMITMENT

The commitment piece of the puzzle may be the most difficult for us to achieve in today's fast-paced world. As we struggle to find time in our already overloaded schedules, making a commitment to our goals is easier said than done. To avoid drifting off course, set small tasks each day which lead you toward your goals and then commit to doing that task and making progress. Do you remember listening to family stories as a kid and how someone was always saying that they were going to get them on paper before they were lost? Did the stories get written down? Probably NOT. Why is that? The answer is plain and simple: no one made a commitment to that goal with timeframes. We cannot kid ourselves that we can set a goal and think about it every day, yet make no

forward progress. To accomplishment anything in life action is required, so don't let yourself off the hook. Get started, work at it, and above all get it done.

"COMMIT"

ALIGN GOALS

This step is one that takes time and a lot of effort. Like many of you, our family has a lot of goals. We had to align these goals so that we could focus on our long-term destination. We had to stop moving in so many different directions all at once and spreading ourselves too thin. The most important realization we came to was that each of us only has 24 hours in a day, so we must use each second wisely. We found that by aligning our goals so that one built on the other we could focus on a few goals at a time and gradually build toward our destination. One other thing to be conscious of is that the daily tasks you undertake are leading you toward your goals and not just keeping you busy. For example, if you want to start an Internet Business and you run around meeting with graphic designers and consultants but never really decide what product or service you are going to sell, then this is just busy work. Decide what your goals are before you take action or you may find yourself running around doing meaningless activities which do not get you closer to your goal.

FLEXIBILITY

Your goals have to have a certain amount of flexibility. There will be times you completely underestimate the amount of time it takes to accomplish something and when that happens you have to be able to decelerate the timeline but still make good progress. Conversely, there will be times you set a goal expecting it to take six months and suddenly it happens in six weeks. This is fabulous! At these times you have to accelerate your goals rather than rest on your laurels. Keep pushing yourself.

The biggest mistake that we can make is to see *goals* as *tasks*. We need to view TASKS as the small stepping stones on the road to our destination – "OUR GOALS." For example, if your goal is to get a certification to move ahead in your business, then some goal related tasks might be searching out various options to get that certification. As you check off each of the small tasks you move toward your goal. This movement towards your goal gives you a feeling of control and even more importantly a sense of accomplishment. There is one pitfall that everyone seems to fall into from time to time – action or just busy work. What you must ensure is that each task is working you towards that BIG GOAL.

The best thing we have found is to step back on a weekly and monthly basis to evaluate if our ACTIONS have been productive. We have to remember to be honest and to be accountable for our actions – that is the only way we will accomplish the GOALS we have set for ourselves, our family, or our business.

PRIORITIZING GOALS

Today's society has moved towards one that wants everything. Having big dreams is a wonderful thing but what today's society doesn't do well is prioritize what it wants – we just want it ALL! This gives each of us a huge problem: we are only one person and have only so much time each day. So what each of us must do is decide which goals are the most important and which ones should temporarily take a back seat.

We can show you an easy way we were taught to sort your goals and decide which ones go where on your priority list. This exercise involves writing a list of what you consider to be your top 30 goals. Yes, 30. This may seem like a lot but you need at least that many so that you will draw out the good ones – the ones which make your heart skip a beat – so write down everything.

Once you have at least 30, go through the list and take it down to 20; remove the ones that are least important to you – set those aside; they are group three. Now look at the 20 that are left and remove the 10 that are the next least important; they are group two. Now you are down to 10 goals that you believe are the most important to you. These TOP 10 must be ones that you can get emotionally involved with.

The key way to prioritize your TOP TEN is to take a few minutes and close your eyes, focusing on each goal individually. Make notes about how each of them makes you feel. Once you have visualized each goal, which one produces the most emotional charge for you? That is number one. Continue to go down the list and list them in order of your emotional connection, with the most connected at the top and the least

connected at the bottom. These 10 goals are the ones that you actively work on. Do not be tempted to glance over at the goals in your group two or group three. The reasons you will be tempted by the goals in the other two groups is because they are easier or faster. What you need to remember is that they are not what you really want right here, right now. If you allow them to enter your thoughts they will only take up time which can be used to accomplish the tasks that will lead you toward the goals that are really important to you.

Anytime you have a question about which goal or which project should have precedence, go back to the way you prioritized your top 10. Stop for a few minutes, close your eyes and focus on the goal then simply ask yourself which one moves me? That is your answer; now it is your responsibility to take ACTION.

LONG-TERM AND SHORT-TERM GOALS

We all need short- and long-term goals. Our long-term goals are our aspirations and dreams and usually have a timeline of five years or more. Our short-term goals must be seen as the stops along the road to that big overall goal. The timeline for these short-term goals is much shorter, usually six months to a year. The tasks are the weekly or daily "ACTIONS" that accomplish those short-term goals. When you add commitment to the *actions,* your long-term *goals* become your *reality*.

So why not just stick to the big long-term goals and do away with all these short-term goals? The truth is that we all perform better with regular and consistent reinforcement, and we also

JIMMY & LORI GUNSCH

all need to experience *success.* By tracking your progress and seeing your short-term goals accomplished, you begin to sense the long-term goals coming to life. As your long-term goals breathe life, they feel that much closer and easier to reach.

Remember you are always closer than you think!

The long-term goals have a bigger and even more important function than your short-term goals. Long-term goals give you your direction;, they provide a focal point when life gets in the way. You get through the setbacks and hard times by focusing on the long-term goal and visualizing the big picture. Your goals are what will prevent you from quitting, and even more importantly, they allow you to see your setbacks as only temporary. Seeing your situation as temporary gives you the strength to search for solutions. As you overcome each difficulty, you builds the confidence you will need to push on toward that long-term goal.

Now we need to show you how to make your short-term goals be the steppingstones to your long-term goals and thus to your dreams. We feel the best way to do this is to give you an example.

JOE – PROFESSIONAL ROPER

Joe was a professional roper who spent years traveling across the country pursuing his career. After spending so many years on the trail he is looking to make some changes. He wants to give back to the sport he loves by sharing his experience with

the youth of his sport. Over time Joe wants to create a training program that will focus on the mental side of sport. Joe wants to earn more money and the financial freedom to leave the rodeo circuit and focus on the youth while earning a substantial income from his training program.

When Joe imagines these goals, he is emotionally attached to the financial freedom. Joe's goals might look something like this:

Long-Term Goal: Replace income and leave rodeo circuit.

A. Short-Term Goals Related to Long-Term Goal
  - Start Roping Practices
  - Start Roping Schools
  - Create Training Program – Focus on Mental Preparation

B. Weekly Tasks Related to Short-Term Goal
  - Place ads or notices in local arenas and rodeo papers advertising practices and schools.
  - Improve current arena to accommodate the practices and schools
  - Improve yard site to accommodate increase in trucks and trailers
  - Locate a supply of roping cattle.
  - Purchase a practice machine

C. Weekly Tasks Related to Short-Term Goals
  - List the content(outline) of training program.
  - Locate mentors.
  - Investigate format options for Training Program

You can see how the long-term goals and short-term goals are interrelated; they are not separate but support each other.

Do not spend hours, days, and even weeks getting hung up on the details of trying to figure out how to get started achieving your dreams. Follow the blueprint above along with the other information in this chapter and you will have a very easy, workable plan. Decide what you need to do and then start chipping away.

We find the goal setting process to be very motivating. To sustain that motivation, the key for us is to choose goals which are within our realm of control and within a doable timetable. This means we must ensure that the goal we set is correct for us – that it is both realistic but at the same time challenges us.

To ensure you are Setting Effective Goals avoid the following:

UNREALISTIC GOALS

Let's say you decide that you want to make a million dollars and have your own radio show in a year. While you may be able to accomplish both of these goals in the long term, the timetable of a year is probably unrealistic. Another example of an unrealistic goal would be thinking you can lose 50 lbs in a month and keep it off. It may also be a bit unrealistic to think you can make one million dollars in a year in an Internet Business without prior experience. Goals are usually classified as unrealistic because of the timeframe you have placed on them and/or your current skill level. To make the same goals realistic you can change the timeframe and work on your skill level.

UNCHALLENGING GOALS

The opposite of setting unrealistic goals is setting goals that are too low. What you need to realize is that this type of goal is easily attainable and hardly qualifies as a goal at all. Do not try to underestimate yourself or discount the skills you have. As a general rule people become easily bored with a goal that is too easily met. They lose interest and you will too.

You must pick goals that challenge you professionally, mentally, and even spiritually. Go for the ideas that make you stretch your possibilities and require a high level of creativity and energy. You will never achieve great things without pushing yourself. Goals that don't push you move you sideways, not forward. They do not get you out of your *comfort zone* or force you to learn new and difficult lessons. It takes two key factors to reach any goal: seriousness and flexibility.

While it may seem that all this planning and thinking about your goals is a waste of your valuable time – time that could be used more wisely to achieve your goals – planning and thinking about your goals must be seen as the stepping stones to achieving your long-term goals.

Many obstacles can and will get in your way as you strive toward your goals. Knowing what not to do is almost as important as knowing what to do. Learning, especially from others and from mentors, saves time by enabling you to avoid pitfalls others have experienced. Every setback you avoid is time saved toward achieving your long-term goal. Studying where you want to go and how you are going to get there gives you a clear path and helps you avoid problems and make a plan to overcome them.

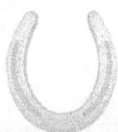

When you are serious about a goal, you take the necessary steps to achieve it. You must give yourself self-imposed deadlines for specific tasks and evaluate your own progress.

We have already said that when you are serious about achieving your goals you must put them in writing. Next you must announce your goals publicly. This is a very scary step for many of us as we see it as an opportunity for those around us to ridicule us in advance. But writing your goal down and then announcing it provides additional motivation since you know people will be asking about your progress. This gives you not only accountability to yourself, but also to others.

When you announce your goals publicly choose your words carefully because they will show how serious and committed you are to these goals.

Read these two examples:

*"I'm going to lose 50 pounds
and run a 10K by this time next year,"*

or

*"After the holidays I'm going to lose weight
and then I'll be able to do what I want."*

Which one depicts someone who is serious and committed? That is who you want to be! Do not procrastinate; do not make wishes that will go nowhere. Every day you waste is a day wasted. You don't get it back and you don't get to try again as that day is gone forever.

"Do not wait; the time will never be "just right."

*Start where you stand and work with whatever tools
you may have at your command, and better tools will
be found as you go along."*

—NAPOLEON HILL
AUTHOR

Something else that we have to keep in mind when setting goals is flexibility. We need to be flexible but that this does not mean giving yourself a break and being lazy. It does mean using creativity to overcome obstacles and listening to feedback, through which you can fine tune your goals as you go. You must have the ability to step back on a regular basis (we recommend at least monthly) and evaluate your progress. What worked? What didn't? What changes are you going to make in your strategy and task list for next month?

Goal planning is risky business. Risky because you could make a wrong move, a bad decision, or even suffer a major setback. Along with that you must still juggle work, family, and bills in addition to striving toward your long-term goals. There are times when certain goals will temporarily take a back seat to others out of necessity, but all of these instances give you the opportunity to be creative and perhaps even come across another opportunity which fits into your long-term goals. This means you also must be adaptable to changing circumstances.

"Progress always involves risks.
You can't steal second base and keep your foot on first."

—FREDERICK WILCOX
WRITER

Feedback is important because no matter how well you have researched or planned, there may be some areas you have overlooked or are unaware of. You may also lose your perspective from time to time and be unable to correctly assess your own efforts. At these times a wise or experienced friend or family member can help you get back on track.

Mentors and mastermind partners who are aware of your goals will also be able to offer encouragement. Talk to them about where you are on the path to your goals, what progress you've made, and what problems you have encountered. They may be able to offer suggestions or solutions.

We can tell you that without the mentors and mastermind partners we have picked up along the way we would have lost our way. To each of them, thank you: we are so very grateful to each and every one of you!

There are times when you may have doubts and these can be compounded by family and friends who may be telling you everything that you can't do and discouraging you from moving forward. You have to remember to focus on your plan. This means not letting negative emotions get the best of you to the point that you 'try to prove everyone wrong.' While harsh comments may motivate you to strive toward your goal, they may also lead you into the pit of self-sabotage. When you allow

others to affect your plan and you try to accelerate it to prove something, you may end up with less than you started with.

You must guard yourself against this kind of reaction. Stick to your plan and avoid the traps. Keep your mind open to receiving all that is available. Build on what you have and learn from each lesson as you make consistent progress. One of Newton's laws of physics is that *'an object in motion stays in motion, while an object at rest stays at rest.'* The same is true for the human mind. If you feel in control and like you are making progress, then it is easier to keep going. However, if you feel out of control and come to a stop, then it takes even more effort to get going again.

No one navigates this perfectly and that's okay – you don't need to be perfect, just committed to having an open heart to receive and you will be given what you need to make your dreams a reality.

> *"Give to the world the best you have,*
> *And the best will come back to you."*
>
> –ELLA WHEELER WILCOX
> POET/JOURNALIST

FIVE

I'LL TAKE TIME MANAGEMENT FOR $100

Everyone gets the same amount of TIME

– NO MORE or NO LESS.

1,440 Minutes per DAY

10, 080 Minutes per WEEK

CHAPTER 5

You have your list of goals, now the panic sets in. The first thought that most of us have is, *"How in the world can I fit any of this into my already packed schedule?"* It is no secret that one of the biggest hurdles that families face today is overloaded schedules. The key is not to become overwhelmed at this point. What each of us MUST realize is that time is the most valuable commodity we have. We can't make any more of it, and once it passes it is gone forever. What we must do is step back and enjoy the time we do have and *choose* to spend that time doing what is important rather than what is urgent.

When you think about and evaluate your day, how many things would you put in the 'urgent' category? When you consider how much time you spend running around doing small items such as going to the bank, post office, grocery store, car wash, and a million other small tasks, it's easy to see why you never seem to have time to accomplish those really important goals.

A false belief that many people have is that once they get to a particular point or achieve a particular goal they will be

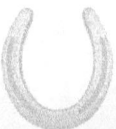

happy. What they find, however, is that happiness isn't a goal; it is what happens naturally on the way to achieving your dreams. It is the journey that brings happiness, not a particular destination. For example, you may think that once you buy your dream home you will be happy. The reality is that the home makes you feel good for a time, but then you will start to want to achieve more. Goals are an ever-expanding set of accomplishments; they don't ever end.

We see this frequently with people who decide to retire. They stop working and for a few months or even possibly a year or two they take vacations, spend time with family, and enjoy life. Then they wake up one morning *bored*. We are all creative beings who need to be challenged and mentally stimulated. So they choose to volunteer in their communities or even go back to work part time. We assume that we work because we have to earn a living, but really most of us work because we enjoy feeling *vital* and *needed*.

YOU CAN'T MANAGE TIME

If you've sat in a corporate office for more than a day, then you know that the idea of time management is everywhere. Everyone wants to know how they can fit more into each day and *wring* every minute out of every hour. Contrary to popular belief, there is no such thing as time management. Time is an unchangeable force and pays no attention to the leanings and desires of mere humans. There is nothing you can ever do to *'make'* more time. The only thing you can do is prioritize activities to accomplish the things that matter most. Time management is about arranging what you do to fit as neatly as

possible into the time you have available. Prioritizing is about focusing only on the tasks that really matter and cutting down the rest or eliminating them altogether.

Most of us see this as budgeting, similar to how a family handles their finances. This is fine as long as you ensure that you are prioritizing, not simply rearranging what you are already doing. Prioritizing will allow you to find the items to be eliminated and then you MUST eliminate. So decide what is important and eliminate what is not! Elimination is key if you are going to make room to accomplish what you really want.

Prioritizing involves making *choices* and *decisions* about every activity that you engage in to see if it adds value to your life or not. A good exercise is to look at your life right now and think about what your family is currently involved in and write it down. Now think about what you want to accomplish and write that down. Is what your family currently doing going to get you what you wrote on your accomplishment list? If the answer is "NO" – you have but one *choice*. You MUST find an hour or two each week to work toward your goals.

Imagine that you are sitting in the doctor's office and he tells you that you have exactly one year to live. How does that change your priorities? Would you try to accomplish your dreams in only a few hours per week? Would you work extra hours to try and get a promotion at work that would never benefit you? Would you save for a retirement that wasn't going to happen? Would you plan to take a vacation for two weeks next June and hope you made it? Would you sit in front of the TV tonight?

Here is a story that sums it all up for us.

*A man lay on his bed at the end of his
life waiting to die...*

*His dream came to pay last respects and bid
farewell to the man who had never used it.*

*As it entered the room the man looked
down in shame.*

"Why did you not realize me?" the dream asked.

"Because I was afraid," the man said.

"Afraid of what," said the dream.

"I was afraid I would fail."

*"But haven't you failed by not attempting
to use me?"*

*"Yes, I did, but I always thought there
would be tomorrow."*

*"You FOOL!" said the dream. "Did it never
occur to you that there was only ever today? The
moment that you are in right now is it! Do you
think that now that death is here you can put it off
until tomorrow?"*

*"No" said the man, a tear gently rolling
down his cheek.*

*The dream was softer now because it knew that
there were two types of pain, the pain of discipline
and the pain of regret; while discipline weighs
ounces, regret weighs pounds.*

Then the dream leant forward to gently wipe away
the tear and said, "You need only have taken the
first step and I would have taken one to meet you,
for the only thing that ever separated us was the
belief in your mind that you couldn't have me."
Then they said goodbye and they both died…

When we feel like we have a seemingly unlimited amount of time, it's so very easy to waste it. When your perception is altered and artificially shortened, we then see time as very precious. The point is that time is always *precious*. Whether you live to be 40 or into your 90s, there is still only a limited amount – and it will never seem like enough. That is why it is so very critical to prioritize what you do each day.

Do NOT let LIFE pass in a blur of busyness that never accomplishes anything.

In order to begin the process of prioritizing, you must learn to look at every activity in your life in relationship to time. Often people don't even think about money in relation to time, but we must realize that they work hand in hand.

Many of us are infatuated with the concept of a *'deal.'* We want to get the best price for anything and everything and convince ourselves that we must do so in order to make our money stretch as far as possible. What many don't realize is what this *mindset* costs in relation to the time it takes. For example, have you ever driven across town to save an extra three cents on gas? Phoned the bank and waited on hold for over 10 minutes to protest a $2 fee you don't recognize? Searched online for hours for the best price for a flight? You

might argue that these activities are what any responsible person would do. Is it responsible to place such a low priority on our MOST valuable commodity – TIME?!

Your vehicle holds 60 litres of gas, and you drive across town to save $.03 per litre. This takes you thirty minutes. You saved $1.80. Now if someone were to call you and offer to pay you $4 per hour for your time you would be insulted. Yet that is want you just demonstrated your time to be worth.

If you call the bank to save $2 and wait 15 minutes, then you are worth $8 per hour. If you search three hours online to save $30 on airfare, then you are worth $10 per hour. But wait, there's more to it than that. Not only are you devaluing your time to a ridiculously small amount, you are also experiencing what is known as *"opportunity cost."* This cost is the price you pay in lost time for being unable to fully implement ideas that earn passive income, or to put off implementing them because you think you don't have "time."

For example, let's assume you have a great idea for a website that produces income by providing readers timely newsletters and articles on parenting. You want to get the idea up and running but don't think you have 'time' because you are so busy. So you wait. First one year goes by and then two. Finally you get things underway and the website grows over the next year to produce $5,000 per month in subscription and advertising revenue. Now it is easy to look back and see what all those busy activities were actually costing you. Things like hanging out with coworkers, chatting on the phone, watching television, texting your friends, surfing the Internet, and volunteering for committees. You felt busy – too busy in fact to insert a new business into your life –

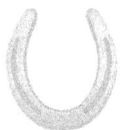

but what did all that busyness get you in relation to what it cost by delaying this idea?

Another great time-waster that people frequently engage in is the old *"what-if"* game. They worry about the mights and maybes. They rerun past events through their minds repeatedly, wasting the present. There is a quote by Mark Twain that we like which says, *"I am an old man and have known a great many troubles but most of them never happened."* The same is true for you if you engage in a great deal of emotional drama about things that are *unknown* or that have *already happened.* You create troubles in your mind that have nothing to do with reality and waste precious time.

Time is very precious something that has come to the forefront in our family this year, We have had to take a long hard look at it as we saw many friends face some of these exact situations.

The hard truth is that no one knows how much time we will be given on this earth so we have to make the most of each and every day! *Balance* is what we have learned over the past year. Set priorities that create that *balance* – money is the fuel of life but you cannot take it with you. The same can be said of time, so use it very wisely. Do not work your whole life without doing some *living.* Do not let saving money or being cheap keep you from doing the things you want to do!

Live today because tomorrow never comes!

BUSY OR NECESSARY?

It is easy to assume that if a task takes a great deal of time it is important. One of these might be keeping up with friends on the Internet or by phone. Yet what do you talk about with these friends? Rarely are our conversations little more than *chatter,* yet we spend huge amounts of time communicating although we aren't saying much. Very few things are truly important or urgent, yet we get so wrapped up in the idea of instant communication, we perceive them to be of vital importance and 99% of the time they just aren't.

Technology has made our lives much easier in a number of ways, but the idea that anyone can contact you at any time, for anything, allows many people to waste your time with unimportant questions or needs. This is one of the reasons that the first person most business people hire is an assistant to deal with phone calls, email and correspondence. When you look at your family, you can see it is like running a small business in miniature. If you waste all your time doing administrative type tasks, then who does the important tasks, like raising your children? Keeping up with people and activities is incredibly time consuming and needs to be done but is not near important enough to take you away from much more important activities.

"You cannot be really first-rate at your work,
If your work is all you are."

–ANNA QUINDLEN
ESSAYIST/NOVELIST

THE PARETO PRINCIPLE

Almost anyone with a management or economics background has heard of *The Pareto Principle*. This principle was first suggested by Joseph Juran who was a leader in management theory. He suggested that 80% of your results come from just 20% of your efforts. This concept is very useful when evaluating your daily activities. One task that we've heard suggested for those trying to prioritize their life is to keep a log of every single activity that you engage in during the day and find the 20% that is producing the vast majority of your results. Once you identify these important tasks, take a look at all the others. It is this list that you will *reduce* or *eliminate*. Most people find that there are easily 10% of their activities wasting enormous amounts of time – these should be completely eliminated. The remaining tasks should be consolidated and reduced to a specific timeframe or delegated to someone else. For example, do you really need to go to the grocery store three times per week when once will do and allow you to spend more time with your family?

It is much better to be extremely selective of where you put your energies rather than allow yourself to be spread too thin. Then you will be able to *focus* on the tasks that help you reach your goals quickly rather than delaying your *success*. While you may feel you lack sufficient time, you must take responsibility and know that it is really just a lack of priorities.

Once you make your list of activities you may be surprised to learn how much time you spend on things that are unnecessary or accomplish nothing. Don't be too hard on yourself. We are trained from childhood, now more so than

ever, to fill every waking moment with an activity. We don't like being bored and our minds need stimulation. The problem this has created is that we do not actively think about or choose the type of stimuli we let into our minds. We must actively *choose* positive stimulation and avoid inventing distraction.

The ability to effectively prioritize the activities of each day requires that you value your time. It's a basic self-esteem issue. If you see your life as valuable and meaningful, then you will value your time as well. If you find yourself wasting a lot of time, you probably don't have a strong enough reason to manage your activities in the best possible way. If your life has no meaningful purpose or direction, then it is unlikely that there will be a compelling reason to change. You might get motivated on occasion, but your motivation to improve just won't last. It is important to remember in raising children that they mirror what they see in us.

> *Do you really want unmotivated, unhappy*
> *children who don't value themselves?*

You must find your purpose first or any attempt to prioritize activities will be in vain because you have no *crystal clear* picture. Once you understand your purpose you can begin to create actions that align with it, but realize that prioritizing your activities requires that you decide what to do and then take action. Most tips and advice that you hear on time management focus on getting things done. But if you haven't decided on the best course of action then engaging in a bunch of activities just makes you feel busy; it doesn't accomplish anything.

Some of you may have experienced this frustration. You feel like you know your purpose but continually *spin your wheels* trying to accomplish it. This could be because your conscious mind feels your new ideas and purpose are correct, but your subconscious hasn't accepted them yet. This is seen all the time when people read a book or attend a seminar and decide they want to change. Instead of focusing on what got them to their current place – their beliefs – they start by changing their activities. They recognize something isn't working, but instead of resolving the conflict, they try to avoid thinking about it. They go through at least one and sometimes numerous unhealthy cycles of hiding the truth from themselves. In order to move forward with purpose they need to stop hiding and be honest with themselves.

> *"In MINDS crammed with thoughts, organs clogged with TOXINS, and BODIES stiffened with neglect, there is just no space for ANYTHING else."*

> —ALISON ROSE LEVY
> JOURNALIST/COACH

REAL PROGRESS

The main objective is to make the greatest amount of progress toward your goals with the least amount of effort. There are numerous methods out there that you can use to achieve this objective. There are a few common threads to all of them:

1. *Purpose* – In order to effectively prioritize you must know your purpose or objective. If we think about our purpose in relation to climbing a mountain, it is important to focus on getting to the top of the mountain. This does not mean you go around it or focus on camping at the base of the slope. You focus on reaching the peak and compare all your tasks to that one objective; the tasks that move you furthest and fastest toward that purpose go at the top of your list.

2. *Time* – As we've already discussed, time is your *"hottest"* commodity because you cannot ever create more of it – your *scarcest resource*. Keep the following in mind as you evaluate the time it will take to complete each task in relation to the amount of forward progress you will make. The tasks that propel you forward in the least amount of time with the greatest reward are ranked higher. At the same time, it is also important to take into consideration how flexible that time is. Can you perform the task by utilizing short amounts of time which can be rearranged at will or does it require a set amount of time and performance in a set location?

3. *Other resources* – You also must evaluate the amount of other resources that a task takes to rank it even more specifically. These resources include things such as *money, family time, use of social network,* and *physical energy.*

The method we like to use is to simply create a list of the top five things at the end of each day that we want to accomplish the next day. We keep the above factors in mind when making the list. This allows us to focus on the absolutely essential tasks at the beginning of the day, and if something doesn't get done, it will be the tasks at the end of the list that aren't as critical. It doesn't have to be difficult or complicated. We know that the important concept here is to understand the need for a clear way to rank what we do each day; then it is up to us to take the required "ACTION" to accomplishing those tasks.

MAKING THE DECISION

> *"In every success story, you find someone who has made a courageous decision."*
>
> —Peter F. Drucker
> Management Consultant/Author

Decisions are all about *choice* and *evaluation*. At times we have numerous options presented to us to accomplish the same task. We have to make a *choice*, a *decision*. This is relatively simple and can be evaluated using the prioritization strategy we just talked about to determine the best option based on the given criteria. But there are other decisions which are harder to evaluate.

The tough *choices* are the ones that involve one or more unknown. We can't know in advance what the consequences of each alternative will be and we can waste precious time trying

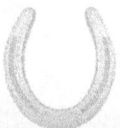

to guess. When you spend time trying to determine all the consequences, a great deal of time is lost and time stagnation occurs. This is especially true for what we perceive to be the *"BIG"* decisions like quitting a job, starting a business, or moving to a new city for better opportunities. There is no way to know all the determining factors before leaping into the unknown.

What people often do in such situations is experience an extended type of *mental paralysis*. The fear of the unknown allows them to put off any *decision* and *procrastinate*. Every decision involves a *choice* between maintaining the status quo of your existing beliefs versus making a change. Because you can't guarantee a particular change will work out for the better, by default you stay put.

> *"Our doubts are traitors and make use lose the*
> *good we oft might win, fearing to attempt."*
>
> **—WILLIAM SHAKESPEARE**
> **POET/PLAYWRIGHT/ACTOR**

You will need to set aside that little voice in your head that keeps saying *'what if this or what if that.'* You cannot let your existing beliefs sabotage your dreams. When you can do this you will be making decisions very quickly– even the *"BIG"* ones. Decisions are actually a form of self-expression of who you are and what your purpose is. Each one confirms the beliefs you have about yourself and the direction in which you are traveling.

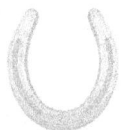

Another reason we procrastinate on projects is because we don't know where to begin. A goal like ' *writing a book*' might seem straight forward enough when the goal is first set, but when it comes time to act, the goal becomes a huge pit of unknowns. Procrastination soon follows. One way to get beyond this is to focus on the step right in front of you. Once that step is complete, you move on to the next step. For example, if you were writing a book about dieting, the first step would be to create a very simple outline that lists the content of each chapter. Once that is done, the next step would be to take the title of chapter one and list fifteen ideas that explain that chapter. The next step would be to list those ideas in logical order and then spend five minutes writing on each of the fifteen items.

By focusing on each step rather than the project as a whole, each portion comes together in a logical fashion and removes the overwhelming feelings associated with the idea of "*writing a book.*" Breaking big concepts and decisions into little concepts and choices allows you to focus and make progress rather than procrastinate because something seems too big for you to accomplish.

One solution that some people find effective is to break a large project down into a lengthy list of small steps, planning it all the way from beginning to end if possible. These small steps are very basic action items, so small in fact that you'd be hard-pressed to break them down any further without it being ridiculous to do so.

You may be thinking that it isn't always possible to break a large project down into small steps before you start. However by breaking it down you will sometimes find that another person may have already done most of the work for you, so take advantage and don't reinvent the wheel. For example, if you want to know how to write a book, you can find books with step-by-step instructions on how to do so. I wouldn't say they break it down all the way to the level of these small steps, but they do come close and give you wonderful guidance to get started.

Then there are indeed situations where there's simply too much uncertainty to plan a project from beginning to end with any level of specificity. A good example is website development, which often works best with an interactive process. In such situations, you can still use small steps to plan out as far as you can reasonably see; then when you reach a certain milestone, update your plan for the next stretch ahead.

It really doesn't matter what path you choose as long as you have some way of prioritizing your tasks and evaluating your choices. A proper plan with the right level of subdivision for where you are at on the path can be very motivating.

> *"Successful people make decisions quickly*
> *and change them slowly if and when at all."*
>
> **—NAPOLEON HILL**
> **AUTHOR**

ACTION IS EVERYTHING

Once you have a *crystal-clear* picture – your purpose – you must take *"ACTION."* By completing those first few steps, you prove how really serious you are.

By creating a task list for a project, you separate the planning from the doing. The task list allows the action phase to go more smoothly and move you towards your goal. What you will discover is that if you follow your plan, you're going to get a result. What we know is the journey may not be smooth or perfect but you will reach your destination.

> *"If we fix a GOAL and WORK towards it,*
> *Then we are never just passing TIME."*
>
> **—ANNA NEAGLE**
> **ACTRESS**

SIX

THE TROUBLE WITH MONEY

*"You are not your job, status, or bank account;
you are who (ever) you think you are."*

CHAPTER 6

In the current economic times it easy to see why money is the number one stressor of couples and families. Anyone who has ever been faced with trying to make ends meet will attest to this. What most people don't realize is that *money* isn't the real problem at all. The real issue lies in what we *think* and possibly even more significant, in what we *feel* about money. When we take a look at our finances objectively we realize there are things we feel we 'must' pay for. The question is, *"Why do we feel that way?"* Ask yourself: *"Why do I feel I must drive a certain car or live in a certain location?"* Could it be that we see the things we possess as a way of keeping score of *'how well we're doing'*? That being said, it would it be safe to say that we see our possessions as proof of our status and accomplishments.

If you believe that you are in no way affected by money or status, ask yourself: *"How would I feel if I suddenly lived in a huge mansion?"* or *"What if I was suddenly homeless?"* Would you feel happy, out of place, guilty, proud? These *emotions are what* underly the issue we have with money. Not having enough money can create feelings of fear, anger, shame, and anxiety, among many others. Having plenty of money can create

feelings of pride, joy, entitlement, obligation and burden. It is all about how we *FEEL*. The key to controlling how and what we feel about money is to control our thoughts about money!

How each of us react to these circumstances is distinct because the emotions we attach to these monetary events are different. These emotions are diverse because each of us has been conditioned by the environments we have been exposed to. This detail is important to understand because just like you received your DNA from your parents, your current ideas about money, finances, and household management also came from your parents. That being said, it follows that the ideas you currently have on these subjects are being passed on to your children. The one thing every parent knows is that our children are always watching and listening to us – even if it is hard to believe at times. Our actions in most situations are what our children use to determine how they should or shouldn't handle things. In today's world, wealth and status seem to be more important than they were in the past. The result is that children watch as their parents literally tie themselves in knots to achieve what they believe wealth and status will give them. Families today find themselves signing their lives into *slavery*, buying the next biggest and better thing, trying to keep up with what they think is accepted. Getting these *financial demons* under control must be seen as a major priority for families in any economy, but especially in today's atmosphere.

The good news is that we all have the ability to change what we currently believe about money; the choice is ours. The key to this change will be to develop a healthier and more objective viewpoint about the role money plays in our lives.

Most of us have been programmed to see someone who has a lot of material wealth as someone who must have had special knowledge or connections to be able to live in that world. It can be easy to think that wealthy people have a natural talent for growing money, but that is not always the case. There are many examples of wealth squandered by individuals who had no knowledge of how to handle money when they inherited it. They never learned anything about money and they weren't born with specialized knowledge. Then there are the people who seem to accumulate wealth so easily that they can be viewed as *"lucky."* These people did not have fate on their side and were not destined to have money; they merely developed the *mindset* and the *skill* to make it look easy.

What we need to avoid is constantly comparing ourselves to others to get our idea of where we fit in the world. When we do this, it unfortunately it gives us the idea that we are less than someone else, which is absolutely not true. We are equal to any other person and they are equal to us. There is no shortage of success or wealth; there is an abundant supply to go around and you don't have to be special or privileged to achieve great things. Every single person has the same potential and the only differences are the ones we perceive in our minds.

> *"The world is full of abundance and opportunity, but far too many come to the fountain of life with a sieve instead of a tank car, a teaspoon instead of a steam shovel. They expect little and as a result they get little."*

> —BEN SWEETLAND
> AUTHOR

This is especially true with young children. What you believe about yourself and your potential stems from a collection of experiences and statements that you took in as a child. All of us remember a child from school who was repeatedly labeled slow or stupid. Years later we attend a school reunion or read in a local paper about how this person has accomplished some milestone. Why does this happen? The most likely theory is that something happened in their life to change their beliefs about themselves, allowing them to achieve their potential. The other not so likely possibility is that they never believed what was being said about them. Either explanation points to one common thread – *their belief in their own potential*. So in order to achieve great things for yourself and your family as a unit, you must understand and believe that you have the same potential that everyone else has and you must commit to develop that potential.

> *"You are God's highest form of creation.*
>
> *You are a living breathing creative magnet.*
>
> *You have the ability to control what you attract into your life."*
>
> —BOB PROCTOR
> AUTHOR/SPEAKER

Every single person who achieves financial security follows a slightly different path or game plan. They are their own person with their own passions, which are different from yours. This is why you cannot try to imitate what someone else

is doing because you can never imitate their passion; to do so is to doom your own efforts to failure. You must find what you feel passionate about and focus your efforts in that area.

It is easy to understand the possibility of change in your mind, but unless you make a commitment to overcome the beliefs you have developed over the course of your life, you slide back into the same routine life. If you want to build a better life for you and your children, the time to take action is now.

THE LAW OF ATTRACTION

> *"All human thought has a tendency to form itself into its physical equivalent."*
>
> –NAPOLEON HILL
> AUTHOR

The *"The Law of Attraction"* is the most powerful of *"The Universal Laws"* and without question the most famous. If you are anything like we were prior to starting this journey, you may question ever hearing about it. The idea that we could attract what we wanted into our life was a great concept, but a huge leap for us. However as we learned and more importantly began to understand the *law,* we realized it had always been at work in our life. We were just completely unaware of it or sometimes had simply called it by a different name – *"Karma"* or *"Fate."*

The basic explanation of this *law* is that everything that comes into our lives has been attracted by our thoughts – thoughts become things. *"The Law of Attraction"* is always at work and everything that happens to us – good, bad, or indifferent – we have attracted through our thoughts. Like the laws that control gravity here on earth, *"the Law of Attraction"* can never be turned off. We have already touched on the power that your thoughts and beliefs have on your actions and how they affect your mind. *"The Law of Attraction"* deals with how these thoughts affect the world around you.

While the concept that your thoughts attract things into your life sounds quite simple, it requires a heavy dose of personal responsibility. In order to attract the positive results and wealth that you desire, you must first understand that you have attracted every result in your life. Like the Genie says, *"Your wish is my command."* To use this law to its full potential you must be willing to accept full responsibility and blame for your life to date. You can no longer blame others or fate, and you must accept that your own thoughts and beliefs are responsible for your current results.

> *"Any circumstance cannot become your circumstance unless they are invited by you through thought!"*
>
> —BONNIE HARRISON
> AUTHOR/COACH/SPEAKER

With that being said, there are a few important things to remember about *"The Law of Attraction"*: it does not discriminate or judge and it does not have an opinion. What

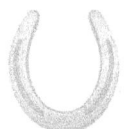

it does do is give you what you focus on – not what you say you want, but what you focus on. It can create good results or it can create bad results in equal measure. Remember the earlier technique where we told you that you should *focus* on what you want to happen rather than focusing and worrying about something negative, like all the bills you have? The reason this is important is due to *"The Law of Attraction."* The more you worry and focus on your fear that you will not make enough money, the more likely it is that you will not make enough money to pay all those bills. By focusing and creating more prosperity in your life, you will attract the solutions and answers that will provide more income. The result is that you will have enough money to take care of any expenses you have without your worrying about them.

In order for you to use *"The Law of Attraction"* in your favor rather than against you, you must first take a good hard look at your present results. This doesn't mean you should feel bad about them – since we know that feeling bad will just attract more of the same. You must do the best you can to take an objective look. Ask yourself: *"What kind of friends do I currently have? What kind of coworkers? How do I feel about my level of income? How is my business going?"* As the answers to these questions flash through your mind, write them down. It is important to write the first answer that pops into your head, not the edited version that comes later. As you look at your list, realize that these ideas are responsible for programming your past and present. Your initial thoughts are a reflection of your subconscious beliefs and are responsible for attracting your current reality. Every result in your life is magnetized to a specific thought and belief that you have.

JIMMY & LORI GUNSCH

"All things are possible to Him who believes."

"The Law of Attraction" is a very simple concept; the difficulty lies in putting it into practice in our daily lives. We know intellectually that this makes good logical sense. We've heard the same basic information from various sources. Yet our results may indicate that we really never understood it to the point of incorporating it into our lives.

This happens for a number of reasons. The first step for most of us is the hardest – examining our results. This self-evaluation can be a very painful experience, so painful in fact that it can stop us cold. This is because when we really take a good look at our life for the first time, knowing we created that life and are responsible for it, it hurts to look at a disappointing result and accept blame for it, and few people have the strength it takes to work though their old beliefs. Those who see it as too much to handle pack it in and as a result they never really make a choice to change. What this group fails to consider is that by doing so they are still invoking *"The Law of Attraction"*, only in a negative and destructive way.

After you take stock of where you are and more importantly take responsibility for what has produced your results, only then will you be truly ready to move forward.

Next you will need to look at the outside influences in your life. The quickest way to derail this journey is underestimate the power of what we come in contact with each day. Every person you spend time around and everything you see and

hear from television or just random conversations has an effect. When we place ourselves in situations and associate with people who have a negative *mindset* it makes it very difficult to stay positive. We all have someone in our life who is constantly spouting a stream of negative thoughts – complaining about their job, their relationships, their lack of money. What you need to be aware of is that if you spend time with this person it will adversely affect your ability to stay positive. It will also affect your physical self – time spent with negative people will leave you feeling physically drained. What happens is they suck the positive energy right out of you!

The only sure way to correct this problem is to stay away from such people, although that is not always an option if they are family members or business contacts.

Here is what we do when faced with this situation: Our first goal is to protect ourselves by not becoming emotionally involved in what they are saying. We refuse to console or sympathize with this type of person, which lessens the impact of their negative thoughts and allows our positive vibration to shine through.

As parents we must be aware how someone else's negativity affects our children. It is up to us as parents to protect our children and in some cases remove them from these situations – especially if the person is an authority figure. There are many teachers, ministers, and even grandparents who are extremely negative and this can really impact your child. We must talk to our children and help them understand how to protect themselves from negative people when we can't be there.

Look back at your responses to the questions we asked about your life and think back to where those ideas originated.

Were they something you heard or experienced in childhood? Are they the words or statements of a teacher, parent, or other influential person? Are they the result of an encounter with a boss, spouse, or former spouse?

Then ask yourself: *"Do I want to continue to allow their thoughts and ideas to control my results?"*

To make progress towards a new *mindset* you must recognize where the thoughts that created your results came from, and choose to change those thoughts. To achieve that new *mindset* you must make a strong commitment to see the change through.

IT TAKES EFFORT

Thinking positive will not be enough – like most things in life it takes effort. Your old beliefs are very strong because they are not made up of only one element. They are a combination of your thoughts, memories, pains and emotions, as well as pictures of people and places and events. As if your thoughts were not enough, add an entire group of habits which support these thoughts. It is because of this multi-layered and complex construction that *"think positive"* programs don't work. You can't apply a *quick fix* solution to a complex problem. On top of that, when you are in a relationship, not only do you have your beliefs about money to work through, you also have the beliefs and issues of your spouse.

When you decide to start looking at the root causes of your money issues, it is essential that you not only look at where you got your beliefs, but where your spouse got theirs.

We came across this analogy the other day and thought how most humans could easily be substituted for the cows and crabs.

COWS AND RHINOS

The cows are happy in the pasture with its fences to keep them safe and secure. The rhinos stay outside the fence and seek freedom by going into the jungle, through the swamp to the warm blue waters and white sandy beaches of paradise.

The cows are a lot like blue crabs; they don't want any others to escape. This is known as the *"phenomenon of the blue crab."*

If you have one crab in a basket, a lid must be kept on the basket to prevent the crab from escaping.

Once you have two or more crabs in the basket the lid can be left off. This is because when one crab tries to escape the other crabs pull it back down.

When one lone crab tries to escape he has no one to pull him down and back into the basket.

The crabs in the basket and the cows in the pasture will ultimately end up on the table.

The crabs and cows that risk escape see the door to opportunity opening. These brave few will not fall into paradise overnight but will have a renewal of the lost hopes and dreams of their youth.

Escape and renew your hopes and dreams – don't allow others to pull you back!

Become a "RHINO."

One of things that continues to astonish us is how little people know about their finances. In a world where money is such a huge issue for families, why is it that so few choose to educate themselves? This is the age where any information we could possibly imagine is but a *"GOOGLE"* away – information which can help you understand how interest works, what investments can do, and how to save for retirement. As parents it is imperative that we not only educate ourselves but also take time to educate our children. Some people shy away from teaching their kids basic monetary skills because they think children shouldn't worry about these things. The reality is that money is the fuel of our financial existence and thus a basic life skill, so parents not teaching their children about money is comparable to not teaching them how to read and write. What we have come to understand is that people fear things they do not know or understand – children are no different. So the best advice we can give in this situation is talk to your children about mortgages, savings accounts, and car loans. Teach them the basic ideas, and instead of being fearful when these items are discussed they will come to see them as just a part of life.

On our journey we came across the following activity, which we have implemented with our daughters to educate them on some key money principles. We have talked about how important it is that children learn all they can about money.

It is titled: Learning about SAVING!

Our goal was to show our daughters how things work in the real world, while keeping it simple.

First we talked to them about the principle of savings – we used the example of purchasing a pack of gum a week. The

lessons turned to things like ensuring they had enough gum to last all week, the consequences of chewing all their gum in one or two days, and sharing the gum if one of their friends came to visit.

We then moved to how this related to their allowance, discussing the kinds of things they would spend their allowance on. The key was to listen to what they were telling us. It was easy to identify the items that held more importance to them, where their "heart" was – it was evident in their voices and faces.

The lesson then moved to the cost of the items they had talked about – how some were inexpensive, others a little more, and some very expensive. We then related their items to things in our world – a night out at the movies, a new car, and a new house.

The next step was to get them thinking about helping others. We focused on things like how fortunate we are, how important it is to be grateful for what we have and to always find something to give to others.

As a result our daughters divide any money they earn or receive as gifts into three categories:

#1 Short Term – Items they want for themselves in the near future.

#2 Long Term – Larger/Expensive items that will take some time to save for – items that could be used to make them money.

#3 Donation Money – Money to donate to help others or use to purchase something for someone else.

We can tell you that this has been a valuable exercise for our girls – they have developed a new sense about money and how we use it every day.

> *"Money is like manure; it's not worth a thing unless*
> *it's spread around encouraging young things to grow."*
>
> –THORTON WILDER
> NOVELIST/PLAYWRITE

NOVELIST/PLAYWRITE

This entire process is likely to take a bit longer than you think it should, but things worthwhile usually do. When we looked back at things we have accomplished in the past, there was always a price to pay. This will be no different for you; to keep your commitment and accomplish this goal you will have to stay focused, invest some time, and pay a price. For each of us the price is different – missing a few soccer games, a favorite TV show, or even a night out with friends. However once this becomes a priority, something that you are determined to achieve, you no longer care or think about what you are giving up. This is known as disciplined repetition. If you want to have a happy home life, getting your finances in order and educating yourself must be your number one goal.

In our daily routines we have a list of things that we determine to be "urgent" and allocate as much time humanly possible to them. This is the level of importance you have to apply to developing a new understanding of money. If you don't allocate time to take care of financial issues, things will

remain exactly as they are right now. However if you are really committed to changing for the better, then you will also shift your priorities to devote the necessary time.

> *"Every worthwhile accomplishment has a price tag attached to it. The question is always whether you are willing to pay the price to attain it – in hard work, patience, faith, and endurance."*
>
> –JOHN C. MAXWELL
> AUTHOR

Your world will open up with every specific new idea or positive belief that you incorporate. As the benefits of these positive actions spill into every area of your life, a very rewarding thing will happen: you will begin to inspire others. It begins with those closest to you as they witness your transformation and grows from there. The way you live your new life will not only effect positive change for yourself, but also for your family and future generations.

Most people see *"someday"* as a place where their dreams will finally come true, and we have to confess there was a time we saw it the same way. What we have learned is that idea of *"someday"* is a killer of possibilities and destroyer of dreams. We knew that if we delayed this any longer our family would be missing out on a lot of what life has to offer. So please remember that the decisions you make right now will determine your future results. If you delay changing your thoughts and ideas, you will never get to *"someday."*

"We say to our kids, 'Follow your dreams!'...yet we aren't out there pushing to become everything we want to be. We aren't out there chasing our dreams."

—PAUL ORBERSON
AUTHOR

TAKE CONTROL, NO EXCUSES

There is a common conception held by many people that life is predetermined, written in the stars, and can't be changed – as if there is a message written in the stars that says *"This is the way it's going to be and it's not up to me."* This of course could not be farther from the truth. The human race has been blessed with intellectual faculties – they are what sets us apart from the beasts. The power to choose comes to us through the intellectual faculty of *"reasoning"*; it is up to us whether we choose to use it or not. So when people think or say they have no choice in how life happens, it is no more than an excuse to absolve themselves of responsibility for their results. It's easier to blame an outside entity or force than to place the blame where it belongs – firmly on their shoulders. No wonder a passive life develops from this attitude, wherein people wait for fate to find them and just *"happen."* It is much like waiting on that mysterious person to show up and bail you out.

"If you want to be bailed out you have to take action and make a call."

The other bailout used by many people is to wait for some stroke of good luck to present them with *riches*. How many people do you know who are simply waiting to win the lottery? They wait patiently. Years go by before they realize that they have not experienced anything; they have virtually slept through most of their days in the endless routine of work, lunch, dinner, occasional entertainment, television, and rest. Each day is the same boring routine until the days become months and then stretch into years. It is many of these same individuals who often struggle to make ends meet and provide for their families. They sit and wait for something, anything, to happen, and they adopt the *mindset* that it's not in the cards for them to make money or have nice things. They give up on any attempt at bettering their circumstances, and their standard of living *spirals* downward. They become the victim of the events they have attracted with their negative attitude – and as a result their lives become progressively worse.

When people choose to live within the confinements of their old beliefs they experience something very similar. This is most evident when someone presents to them a new and exciting possibility or opportunity. They immediately reject the idea and get as far away as possible, for if they accept this new opportunity for a better life or accept that their current situation is their responsibility, they will not be able to go on as they always have.

In the Western world, where we have been given all these freedoms, it is disheartening to see so few of us exercise them. We have become afraid to believe that a better life *can* be ours; instead we choose *"FEAR."* We prefer to believe that it is not

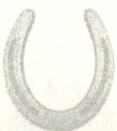

possible and that some outside force such as *fate* is in control. Why? Because to change our lives we must be courageous and fearless – make an effort – and above all make a commitment to change. For many it is easier to stay where they are, blame someone or something else, and tell themselves, *"No, this is too hard. Who am I to think that I can make this happen? What if I fail? Right now, I have something; maybe it isn't the life that I want or even one that I like – but it's mine and I don't want to lose what I have."*

Do not fall into that trap ... choose something better for your life!

Remember, we are each born with an equal measure of potential, and financial prosperity is the birthright of every single person. This does not diminish over time so no matter how old you are you can still tap into that potential that has always been yours. In fact, the more experiences you have had, the more value you can provide for others. We've known numerous people who have had several careers in their lives and this is a great resource to draw from when you are looking for ways to create value.

Nothing happens by chance or accident. The life you have led up to this point may not have produced the results you like, but it can provide the *seeds* for your future as you search for what you are most passionate about. Do not continue to stumble through life hoping for the best. You must actively plan your future and visualize it.

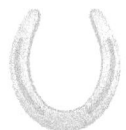

Like us, you will be surprised at the sense of empowerment you will get once you accept responsibility and stop blaming or looking at things like *fate* or *destiny* to explain your life. We have spent so much time floating through our lives without even an idea of where we want to go and recognize this as a complete departure. Your life is completely within your control and the events that you choose to experience are what make you a *unique* individual. Your new sense of empowerment will allow you to enjoy these events more fully as you realize that you created them and now have the ability to create and bring about whatever you desire.

> *"As a creative individual, you will continually attract good things into your life by thinking positive thoughts and expecting the best that life has to offer.*
>
> *You deserve it."*

—BOB PROCTOR
AUTHOR/SPEAKER

SEVEN

TEA PARTIES, MUD PIES, AND FORTS

*"Nothing you do for your children is ever wasted.
They seem not to notice us, hovering, averting
our eyes, and they seldom offer thanks, but what
we do for them is never wasted."*

—GARRISON KEILLOR
AUTHOR/RADIO PERSONALITY

CHAPTER 7

Children are mirrors of our lives. We see it in their play, their words, and their attitudes. While we know that our children learn from us, we sometimes forget that they see the bad habits as well as the good. Unfortunately, we don't get to choose which, as our children observe us 24/7 and learn many things about life from the way we handle the obstacles and challenges in our lives.

One of the top priorities for us as parents is to raise our daughters to be independent thinkers. Not to be afraid to go their own way – to make their own path, to choose the life they want. No parent wants to see their children blindly follow others or think they may not have options and choices in life. We feel the same way and are doing everything we can to ensure our daughters grow up to be independent thinkers.

The biggest challenge for parents is to create a balanced family environment so that their children are comfortable with who they are and are confident in their choices. A child who is at ease with their own sense of who they are as a person will learn to make decisions based on their own *choices*. When they

have no sense of themselves they look to outside factors to guide them – outside influences that may not have their best interests at heart. We know that we are not perfect parents, but we have learned from our own mistakes and the mistakes of others, and are making some rewarding changes for our family. We know we cannot control the actions of our children once they are adults – so we must lay a strong foundation while they are young and give them strong decision making skills so they can face any situation wisely. This is not about judging other parents; it is about us sharing some of the concepts that we have found useful in the hope that you may find them useful as well.

"Every second we live is a new and unique moment of the universe, a moment that never was before and never will be again.

And what do we teach them in school?

We teach them that two and two make four and that Paris is the capital of France.

We should say to each of them, "Do you know who you are?

You are a marvel. You are unique.

In the millions of years that have passed, there has never been another child like you!"

—MOTHER TERESA
HUMANITARIAN

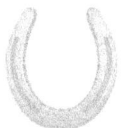

BEHAVIORS MOLD

As parents we have to ask: *"What do we really want our kids to remember about their childhood?"* Stressed parents and crazy chaos, or fun times and enjoying one another? The reality is that parents have tremendous power to shape the lives and beliefs of their children and can show them a great way to live and deal with life.

The best way to accomplish this is by how we react to external influences and events. How we act, feel, and think is crucial because our children see us as the perfect role model to understand how a grownup should react to various situations. If we want children who aren't swayed or devastated by the external, then we can't allow ourselves to be swayed either. Let's face it, we all want to be accepted to some degree by others, but we must be careful that this desire doesn't distract us from our own internal compass.

When we experienced what we considered undeserved ridicule from parts of the rodeo community, it was very hard on us – we felt lost. We knew that our daughters were watching us – learning from how we handled this difficult time. We will be honest – for a time we were very angry but we soon realized that we could not continue on that path. It would have been easy to sweep it under the rug as so many close to us encouraged us to do. but what would that have said to our daughters? We want them to grow up learning that it is OK to stand alone – to go with their principles. In order for our children to learn to stand alone and go with their own principles, we had to do it too. If we're not careful, the behavior we model will reflect an overemphasis on

caring what everyone else thinks instead of doing what we feel is right, and this includes how we handle our own emotions.

Suppressing negative feelings sends children the message that "feelings are very bad and should be buried or hidden." As a result children are reluctant to use their own feelings to guide them in constructive ways. Adults will often take out their own feelings out on others, sending the message that other people are responsible for their feelings and perhaps even their fault. The problem here is that children then learn to use other's feelings as something that steers their thoughts and actions. As parents, we must teach them balance – it is always important to be aware of how others feel and to think but not at the cost of your own feelings and thoughts. We can't allow others to dictate our emotions, and by the same token we are not responsible for the feelings of others. We are only responsible for ourselves and how we react to various events.

The key for us with the rodeo incident was that our girls saw us standing up to be counted and trying to make a difference. In doing so we feel we have shown our girls that no matter what others think or say, you can still move on and be happy in your own life because you know you are doing what is right for you.

CONDITIONS

Another trap parents often fall into is behaving conditionally with their children. Nothing is more powerful in convincing kids to look outward rather than inward for answers. This is why we see so many young people today immediately looking for someone other than themselves to blame. When we learn to look to outward sources for explanations, we take

personal responsibility out of the equation. Most of the time, as parents, we don't even realize that we are promoting this type of attitude. Well-meaning phrases like, *"I love you when,"* and then we go on to list some good things the child does. We may think we are giving our child positive reinforcement; what the child hears is that their parent's love is conditional on them behaving in certain ways. Showing a child love and affection only when they do well enhances their idea that perfection wins love.

Like all parents, we want our girls to strive to be the best they can be. As parents, what all of us need to remember is that they are perfect the way they are and we should enjoy them at every stage of growth. Anyone who has had a small baby can remember wanting them to get to the stage where they sleep through the night or learn to talk or walk. But then when they do, you realize that you didn't really enjoy the stage they were in at the time. We encourage all parents to really enjoy every day with their children and acknowledge how far they have come.

Be grateful for the family that is yours.

FAITH AND TRUST

One thing that is very unfortunate is that within many families there is a common message that parents have little or no faith in their children to make the right *choices.* This is not necessarily because we don't actually have faith in our children, but it is usually more because we don't recognize that they must make mistakes in order to mature. Children learn through trial and error just like adults do, and while it may seem much

easier to just make the decisions for them and save them the heartache, they never truly learn that way. The sad part of this type of scenario is that by controlling every aspect of our children's lives, they can grow up to seek the same environment as an adult, which can be very devastating. As parents we must realize that in most cases more is learned from mistakes than from successes. Allowing your child to choose (within reason, of course) empowers them to trust their own judgment and follow their own path rather than be swayed by others. Of course, this can occasionally produce some interesting and funny incidents, and we all laugh knowingly when we see someone's five-year-old wearing a swimsuit to school under their clothes because we know that parent is allowing their child to choose.

Something that goes hand and hand with faith is trust – as parents we must trust our children. When we show them that we trust them they will go out of their way to prove us right. The same can be said when we do not trust them – they go out of their way to prove us right.

Lori remembers something her parents told her and her older sister as teenagers:

Remember to ask yourself this as you make a decision to do something – "Could I explain my action to Mom and Dad?" You see, they grew up in a small rural community where everyone knew everyone. Lori and her sister realized that it was not "IF" their parents would find out, it was simply a question of "WHEN." By making the statement, the girls' parents felt that they were letting their daughters know they had faith in them to make decisions and trusted that they would be deciding – not blindly following.

PARENTAL HABITS

> *"Your children will see what you're all about by what you live, rather than what you say."*

> —WAYNE DYER
> AUTHOR/SPEAKER

Every parent has their own bad habits when it comes to raising children. In many cases we've inherited them from our own parents or picked them up from some other *'authority'* figure. Have you ever said something to your children and then immediately thought, *"Oh wow, I sound just like my mother (or father)"*? We often fall back on what we have seen and heard in times of stress or anger – *HABITS*. But we can all learn to control how we react and respond. We have listed a few areas that you might like to take a look at and consider how they could be affecting your children.

1. CRITICAL NAGGING

> *"Children need models rather than critics."*

> —JOSEPH JOUBERT
> ESSAYIST/MORALIST

If you are anything like us, we are sure you have found yourself here once or twice. As parents we feel it is our job and duty to instruct our children when they are on the wrong path. This is true, but how we carry out this instruction is crucial to

the development of their self-esteem. Nagging incessantly and being overly critical can convince a child that they are wrong no matter what they do. Not every little thing a child does needs to be harshly corrected. We try to focus on the big things with our children, like always being *honest* and *truthful*. For the smaller stuff like cleaning up after themselves, we show them by example. When issues come up with the smaller things, we talk to them about how everyone in a family has to do their part to keep things running as smooth as possible. In this way they not only learn by our example without nagging, but they are very clear on what the important life skills are and which ones are farther down the list.

2. JUDGMENTS AND EVALUATIONS

Judgments and evaluations represent our own observations and conclusions and we often state them as fact without realizing that since our children view us as an *authority*, they accept those judgments without question. Even off-hand comments can sound like observed facts to a child, statements like:

"Algebra will be very hard for you."
"You're just naturally clumsy. It's not your fault."

*"People like us aren't made for
that type of thing."*

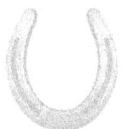

As parents we need to realize what statements like this say to our children – the message is clear that unless they're exactly like us, they're not okay. We knew that is not the message we wanted to send – or that you want or intend to send. Whenever we make assessments or statements about our children, we must be sure to convey that these are opinions, not edicts carved in stone.

3. OVERREACTIONS AND UNREASONABLE PUNISHMENT

"After seventeen years of research and twenty-seven books, I can reduce the keys to raising high-achieving children to three words... "gentle but firm."

–DOUG WEAD
AUTHOR/PHILANTHROPIST/SPEAKER

A warning is used to let our children know that they've strayed off the course we've set for them, whereas a reprimand is the response that lets them know they have arrived at the wrong destination. It can be easy as a parent to let our anger get the best of us, but a habit of overreacting just teaches your children to do the same. The result is that our negative feelings, especially anger and disappointment, can be reflected back to us.

The use of unreasonable punishment can take negativity even further. It's a reprimand coupled with parentally imposed unfair consequences. If your child commits one small infraction but is then sent to their room for hours or made to do some chore for a day, then all it does is focus their anger

toward the parent instead of correcting the initial behavior. We want our children to heed our corrections because they have learned it's the right thing to do, not because they fear some punishment.

Few parents we have ever met have taken any kind of parenting course and that includes us. What we have learned is to keep moving forward to be a better parent. Learn new behaviors that uplift children while still teaching them to be responsible members of society. The best lesson we have learned is to take a deep breath and think before responding to something that one of our children has done or said. When we react instinctually, we do a disservice to ourselves and our children.

4. TEACHING CHILDREN TO THINK

Not only do we have habits that nag our children about how to behave, we also have verbal habits that tell them what to think. If you tell a child not to cry or not to be upset about something, you are discounting their feelings and showing them that they should discount someone else's emotions. It takes patience to ask a child how they feel and why, but it is necessary so they will learn to work through and handle unfamiliar emotions. When a parent tells a child they should be happy when they are not, it confuses them and creates uncertainty about how to feel one way and act another. One great way to teach a child to think for themselves is by asking them questions such as, "*How does this situation make you feel? Why?*" As they talk to you about their feelings, it releases the emotion and helps them understand. This works very well with toddlers, but inevitably resurfaces when children hit puberty.

The teen years are filled with anxiety, new experiences, new relationships, and of course hormones! Teens are very susceptible to what their peers think at this stage and can be heavily influenced by outside forces and events. It is a critical time for the lines of communication between parents and children to be open. Keep those lines open when they are young so that when these critical times come they will be there to put into use.

5. HOVERING PARENTS

There is a fine line between instructing your child and being overly controlling. This is easily revealed when you evaluate how we talk to our children.

For example, do you say things like:

> *"Don't forget your backpack" instead of "Is there anything you're forgetting before the bus comes?"*

> *"You need to wear your helmet if you're going outside to bike" instead of "Biking without a helmet is unsafe."*

> *"Put your jacket on. It's freezing outside!" instead of "It's supposed to get down below zero this afternoon."*

Although it's often easier to tell them what to do, you can only train the brain by either giving them the information that will help them use their own *reasoning* skills to figure things out or letting them suffer logical consequences. There are some situations where suffering the consequences is appropriate, like forgetting their backpack, while other situations are best

JIMMY & LORI GUNSCH

handled by giving them the information to help them make the correct decision, like wearing a bike helmet. And yes, while it's hard to let them go off to school knowing they forgot their backpack, there are times when letting them learn the hard way will have more impact than you constantly trying to help. When we're guiding and disciplining our children, we need to be sure that we're leaving them room to think. To be self-directed, they'll have to come up with their own motives for *behaving, thinking,* and *feeling* a certain way.

6. RESCUING

How many times have you had to make a trip to school because your child forgot their lunch, their homework, or their gym clothes? Have you ever made an appointment with your child's teacher or principle to discuss incidents in the classroom you don't think are being handled properly? It is the instinct of a parent to protect their child. As parents we must recognize when this instinct is not in our children's best interest. In our society it is an all too common occurrence for parents to shield their kids from challenges, settle their conflicts, and rescue them from the consequences of their bad *choices.* We do this because we don't want to look like terrible parents, we can't bear to see them suffer, or we want to avoid conflict. But since it permits them to bypass the *reasoning* process, it further encourages them to hide behind us rather than trust their own *decisions.* What can happen is these children grow to believe that they are not capable of making safe and reliable choices because they were never given a chance to try in the first place.

We all have habits as parents that we don't really even think about most of the time. But it is never too late to change and open the lines of real communication with your child. This means that information and thoughts flow in two directions – not only from the parent to the child. The parent-child relationship can be one of the strongest we ever create, and this requires that we frequently examine our parenting habits and skills to see if they are really helping our children. We feel that no parent intentionally damages their child's self-esteem but we can easily do so without even realizing it.

The good news is that though there are many negative things children sometimes learn from us, they learn many good things as well. As parents we just need to work on ourselves, and this will be passed on to the family.

THE GOOD STUFF

"First we make our habits, then our habits make us."

–CHARLES C. NOBLE
AUTHOR

Here are some of the wonderful positive habits you can instill in your own life and by example into the lives of your children. While many of these you probably already incorporate into your daily habits, we wanted to share with you some of the ways we have been made aware. Some of this newfound awareness led us to educational opportunities for our children so that they too could understand the importance of these principles.

1. BE POLITE

We live in a world of instant communication, texting, and email, and we often forget the simple courtesies that make our day – little things like smiling at people you pass in the mall or saying 'please' and 'thank you'. Children who grow up accepting electronic communication as the *"norm"* often don't realize how important politeness is when dealing with people in person. In fact, politeness is becoming hard to find in our society.

Have you ever opened the door for someone and they walked right through without even an acknowledgement? We have. A simple, "You're welcome," is usually all that is needed to remind someone that they were impolite. As children watch this interaction they become aware not only that it is polite to hold a door for someone, but also that it is rude not to acknowledge someone when they do something nice for you.

In order to have a polite and respectful child, you must be a polite and respectful parent.

2. BE ACTIVE

New reports constantly tell us about the prevalence of obesity and it is a huge concern. When we were in school it was rare to see overweight children – today it is approaching the *"norm."* Our society keeps moving towards more forms of entertainment which separate the family unit, at the same time decreasing activity levels. You only have to ask yourself, *"How many nights per week do I watch TV while my children are in another room playing video games?"* As parents, encourage your children to be active without nagging them by going on

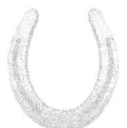

regular family outings that involve all of you. We communicate and relate as a family regularly at rodeos and other events that interest us all and that keep us active. There are so many wonderful activities: horseback riding, hiking, skiing, or just walking the dog, which will allow you to be active as a family and at the same time create wonderful memories.

The greatest thing we began this spring was taking a bike ride up a quiet country road by our house. It is not a long ride but it lets us be active and enjoy each other without interruptions. We read somewhere recently that uninterrupted quality time is more valuable than conditional quantity time. We encourage each of you to turn off your cell phones, TVs, and radios and spend time together – the rewards you'll discover will be beyond your wildest dreams.

3. GET PLENTY OF REST

Once again, the fast pace of our society has seen this critical component take a back seat. Many see rest as a small thing, but getting enough sleep each night is very important to our physical and emotional health. Involvement in activities and other pursuits causes us to deprive ourselves and our children of the much needed rest our bodies require. Most parents can relate to what happens when our children do not get their rest. As adults the scenario is no different – we cannot be at our best when we are *tired*. When our children witness the adults in their lives going without sleep, they think it's normal. Another important issue that is under-prioritized in today's families is a regular schedule of bedtime, not only for the children but for the whole family. Having a predictable habit of sleep allows the

body and mind to recover from the day and actually makes it easier to sleep. We know this can be a huge challenge at times, but it is essential for everyone in the family to be able to function at their highest level.

4. CHALLENGE YOUR MIND

For us this has been the one of the most rewarding discoveries of our journey. Most people's first thought when asked to challenge their mind is to get an education, but it means much more. Individuals who excel in life learn early on to read as an enjoyable activity and this carries over into adulthood. Those who regularly read tend to do much better in school and in higher education. We think it is great for children to see their parents reading and learning no matter what their age. Children can assume that their parent is the absolute authority on everything but when they see them reading and learning they understand that learning is a *lifelong pursuit.* This also lets the children know that no one can be expected to know everything. We see reading – and reading as a family – as a very worthy family activity, one that will see each of you grow as individuals and as a family. As your family learns together you will grow closer in understanding and interests.

As parents we are all required to help our children with their homework. One of the most educational experiences for us was our daughter's book report. She chose a book about Animal Builders – it was a fantastic book and extremely educational – and above all it united us with our daughter. As we took turns reading the book with her, it educated us and gave us a forum to talk with our daughter about something that interested her.

When she presented her report to her class it was rewarding for us to hear how much she learned; better yet was the passion that could be heard in her voice.

5. HONESTY

As adults, we are either in the habit of telling the truth or we're not. We admit that being honest isn't always easy, but we definitely think our kids follow our lead in this area. They watch us and they are very perceptive. They can tell when you embellish a story or pass off a white lie as the truth. We all know people who habitually tell untruths almost without even thinking. This is just a habit which can be often seen as a character flaw by others and which can result in them thinking less of you. This is why it is so very important for your children to understand the importance of telling the truth. They must realize that it is essential not only because it's the right thing to do, but also because of how people will perceive them if they lie. As parents we often punish children for not being truthful, which children can interpret as fibbing being okay as long as they don't get caught. The important thing for us was to get our girls to understanding that lying is wrong whether they get caught or not. Here again, we believe that setting the right example is crucial and adults must focus on being truthful whether someone else knows or not because our children definitely will know.

6. WORK ETHIC

Some people may disagree, but we absolutely believe that work ethic is a learned behavior. We haven't ever seen a child voluntarily clean their room or take out the trash unless they were taught to. When you think about your own life, have you ever had the attitude that something that needs doing isn't your job? Or that you don't get paid to do it so you won't? If this is the case, then how can you expect your children to have a different attitude? There are also parents who do everything for their children and don't teach them how to work.

We had a friend whose daughter had grown up with his ex-wife. He was very concerned that the child would not have any work ethic because the mother doted on her and never asked the child to lift a finger. Sure enough, when she turned sixteen she got a job at a local restaurant. She called her dad that same evening and told him she'd already quit. When he asked why, she replied, "Well they wanted me to clean and stuff and I don't do that. Mom always does it at home."

While it may seem like you are making life easier for your children by not requiring them to do any work, what are you really teaching them about the real world? Sometimes we have to do things we don't necessarily love in order to earn a living, and you can either choose to do these things with a good attitude or you can quit and have no job prospects.

Children learn by our example.

7. GOOD MONEY HABITS

Schools rarely, if ever, teach children sound personal finance principles, so it is imperative that we do so as parents. As with most other habits, actions speak a lot louder than words. Our kids need to see us doing the right things financially so they can follow in our footsteps. This means talking about money in a positive way in front of children so they understand how things really work. Often children only witness arguments about money, and while it is healthy to disagree, financial arguments can make children feel insecure.

It is also important to trust children with small sums of money and teach them how to use that money from an early age.

A single mother we know named Cindy allowed her children (ages 13, 12, and 10) to work around the house for small sums of money. She then used the envelope system we described in the last chapter to teach them to put aside some for savings, some for necessity, and some for donation. Truthfully, all three at one point or another spent everything and then had to be 'broke' for a while to understand how important it was to keep those reserves.

These are lessons easily taught at a young age and habits that will carry forward for a lifetime. Those who don't teach these principles early on may see their children grow up and squander money, run up incredible bills, or even face bankruptcy – all before they are out of their twenties. Though it takes some time, you will save your children a tremendous amount of heartache over the long haul by teaching them early.

8. STAY PLAYFUL

Many parents today are way too serious! It's as if everything they experience is *life* or *death* so their children grow up to be very somber (and often negative) people. The best part of life is living it to the fullest no matter your situation, and even if bad things happen you can still learn to laugh and be fully engaged in adventurous, entertaining, and fun activities. Watch cartoons or play charades and just let go of the stress of daily life. In doing so you are teaching your children that it's okay to unwind and let go of troublesome issues for a time. You should also encourage them to try new things and be adventurous. This includes every area, from traveling to new places to eating new food. If you have ever gone on a cruise as a family, then you know that this can be a great opportunity to try new and different things as well as experiencing new and exotic locations. This type of adventure as a family opens your child's mind to the possibilities beyond what they experience every day and allows them to dream – which is an important part of childhood.

9. ENCOURAGE CURIOSITY

We know that when children are toddlers there are times we wish they'd never learned the word *"Why"* – *Why is the sky blue? Why do ducks quack? Why do trees have leaves?* This natural curiosity is increasingly lost as we age and we can sometimes discourage it in our children. But without curiosity, some of the greatest inventions and discoveries would never have happened. Edison wouldn't have made a light bulb, Columbus wouldn't have discovered North America, and

the wonders of space would have never been explored. Your child may be the discoverer of the next natural wonder or the cure for cancer, but it won't happen unless you as their parent encourage curiosity and engage in it yourself. When is the last time you went to an aquarium or a botanical garden just to learn what's there? Children absorb the world like little sponges and if you present the opportunities they will astound you.

10.   EXERCISE YOUR CREATIVITY

Children are naturally creative. As we grow older, we often lose touch with our creativity, which is sad. Demonstrating to our kids that we have a wide range of interests and helping them learn to express their creativity in increasingly more mature ways is important. If you want to write a book, do it and let you children see you do it. The same is true if you want to learn to speak another language or learn photography. You can even include your children in the process. By allowing them to explore all their interests, you allow them to sample the world and try out many areas. Take them to play golf, ice skate, ride horses, meet authors, visit a house under construction, build a dog house – you limit your child only by limiting your own creativity.

11.   GIVING BACK

This is an area which like simple courtesies is often left behind in our busy world. For us this was very important as we believe that *you get by giving*. As parents we must get our children to see how people in their lives help them each day and how that makes their life better. Ask your children

why they think these people help them; then talk about how grateful they should be for having these people in their lives. It is then important that they realize that sometime people need help in return. Talk to them about how rewarding it can be to help others – for example, helping someone they love like a grandparent. As in everything, it is important that they also see their parents giving back, allowing them to witness how rewarding it can be.

You can teach your children anything by example, be it good or bad, and by consciously choosing the good you can literally change their lives. Twenty years from now they will be emulating the good habits you taught them with their own children rather than the bad habits passed down for generations.

We know that sometimes you don't necessarily feel like you are having any effect on your children but you are because they are watching what you do and say every day. It's up to us as parents to take the lead and teach children how to become happy, satisfied adults and the rewards will be tremendous.

"Always reward your long hours of labor and toil in the very best way, surrounded by your family. Nurture their love carefully, remembering that your children need models, not critics, and your own progress will hasten when you constantly strive to present your best side to your children. And even if you have failed at all else in the eyes of the world, if you have a loving family, you are a success."

—OG MANDINO
AUTHOR

EIGHT

THE SIGNIFICANTS

"A great marriage is not when the 'perfect couple' comes together.

It is when an imperfect couple learns to enjoy their differences."

—DAVE MEURER
HUMOR WRITER

CHAPTER 8

As an adult the most relevant relationship you will have is with your *significant other*. As this will shape a big part of your life, it is key to always be connecting or reconnecting with that person. The early ideas you shared about your life together will be the starting points to determine some mutual goals. It is important to realize goals will change and shift over time, and like a garden, they must be tended carefully. Like your goals, it is imperative that you nurture the relationship with your partner for it to survive and flourish.

One of the biggest contentions between couples these days seems to be the issue of freedom to pursue their own vision or purpose. For many this is seen as selfish or possibly even scary as they watch their partner do their own thing, leaving them behind. What we have come to realize is that done correctly, the opposite actually occurs – the relationship deepens and grows. Selfishness is to expect our partner to do what we want them to do or to be who we want them to be. Each of us here on earth has the right to be who we are and to follow our visions. If you insist that your partner live out your dream, you put them in

the position of having to fight for who they are and what they want. When we do this one of two things can happen: either they grow to resent us or they become a shadow in their own lives – and neither scenario leads to a healthy relationship.

Neither selfishness nor selflessness is good for a relationship because both cost the individuals who they are as a person. Power struggles breed resentment and undermine cooperation in relationships. If one person is giving in or going along with the other to keep the peace, the relationship pays a price. The submissive person is losing himself or herself, and the relationship loses that partner's contributions – in these situations the cost of peace is too high. Both the selfish and selfless persons take away from rather than add to the relationship. There is an old Asian proverb that says, "Two strong people can work out anything." When both individuals in a relationship stand up for themselves, they can work out a solution for what is best for each of them and ultimately for their partnership. Each of us must be allowed to fulfill ourselves; living for our passions and growing as individuals will allow us to make the most of life and add the most to our relationships.

We were all meant to leave our parent's families and to find a spouse or partner with whom to create a new family. If you do not put your partner first you will have compromised your relationship by not committing yourself fully and this can be disastrous. As you grow into adulthood and beyond, it is good to examine and change the beliefs and the values with which you were raised if they don't move you forward in a positive way.

GIVING TO EACH OTHER

"Marriage is not a 50%-50 % thing.

*You must feel like you are giving
60% and receiving only 40%."*

—CAROLINE JOHNSON

For relationships to prosper they must be reciprocal. There are no current ways to objectively measure the give and take in a relationship; our experience is that we each evaluate in our own personal way whether a relationship is balanced by how we feel about what comes back to us from the other person. There is an overall sense of fairness built into us and when the fairness in a relationship is not working, the relationship either changes to correct the imbalance or the relationship ends. If one person feels what is happening is not fair they must insist that the issue be discussed.

What we have found is that it is not always about changing something. In most cases all that is required is a discussion with our spouse which shifts our perspective and then we realize no change is necessary.

What must be avoided is the temptation to withdraw from each other when things aren't going well. It is only by getting the issues out in the open that a solution can be found. -

Another area to address is responsibility and what happens when individual responsibility is not taken in a relationship. This can occur in two ways: one partner doesn't take responsibility, or doesn't allow the other partner to

JIMMY & LORI GUNSCH

take repsonsibilty. Both scenarios have the same result - the relationship suffers.

We all know couples where one partner has health issues and the other partner takes complete responsibility for their partner's health.

Recently we met a couple just like that – the husband had a heart attack and it terrified the wife. The husband, on the other hand, just kept on with life, doing what he had always done, while for the wife it "became her life" – so much so that she lost her perspective and is constantly harassing her husband. This is not a healthy relationship.

In most cases it is imperative that both partners take responsibility for themselves and let the results be their own. This is not always the easiest thing to do but it is in the best interest of the relationship. This advice may seem backward at first, but nagging your partner into compliance with what you want, even if you have their best interest at heart, never works and can do significant damage to your relationship.

You Create Your Experience

Everyone feels *loved* while they are dating and this is what draws them into the relationship in the first place. So when people get married they subconsciously expect their partner to make them feel *loved*. What each of us must realize is that each person comes to the relationship with a different set of *issues* and *problems*. Since no two people are alike this will inevitably bring conflicts which must be worked through and dealt with.

Also, as each of us in a relationship grows as a person we may or may not grow at the same rate as our partner; this occasionally will cause imbalances within the partnership.

Therefore we are teaching our children that it is very important to understand that it is not anyone else's job to make you feel *loved* or to make you *happy*. Loving yourself or thinking highly of yourself is a job you have to do for yourself. Even when someone else esteems or loves you, this is not self-love or self-esteem. You cannot depend on someone else to build you up or make you feel *loved;* if you do you will never create true happiness. Understand that if you climb the elevator with someone else your feelings will go up and down in accordance with their feelings about you. The same can be said when we use external accomplishments such as the car we drive, our salary, and/or our successes to measure our self-esteem. One day your stocks may be up and the next day down; your job and salary can change quickly; you could be a millionaire one day and penniless the next – but you are still the same person. The only steady source of esteem and love is you, and you must be conscious of this and work each day at valuing yourself.

Nobody can make anyone else feel *loved* and no one can make anyone else *happy*. We are all in charge of how loved we feel. If someone else loves you but you don't love yourself, you won't accept their love. If someone else tries to make you happy but you won't allow yourself to feel happy, you will remain unhappy. You choose each and every day if you will be happy or not.

*"Most people are just about as happy
as they make up their minds to be."*

–ABRAHAM LINCOLN
PRESIDENT OF THE UNITED STATES

CHILDREN AND YOUR RELATIONSHIP

Having children and raising good, productive people is one of the main areas of interest for most couples. Like many of you, we discovered that this is much harder than we ever imagined. Once children enter the equation, every belief, idea, or thought process you have seems to be challenged. The challenges don't come only from your children; suddenly your spouse may differ with you on how the children should be nurtured or punished, what kind of rules are appropriate, and even when bedtime is! It is sometimes the smallest items which can cause the biggest gulfs, such as do you open presents on Christmas Eve or Christmas Day? Which set of grandparents are you spend Thanksgiving with, and many other seemingly simple questions.

We have experienced many changes on this journey, but one of the biggest concerned our individual roles within our home. Our roles within our relationship and our family moved away from the more traditional lifestyle of 'stay-at-home mom' and 'bread winning dad' Now that we both have taken an active role in our business, both the business responsibilities and the home responsibilities have to be shared. The road was a little rocky as we worked out our new roles, but through many a discussion we developed a plan as to who would do what. We now have a greater understanding of where the other person is coming from

in any given situation. The plan is working well and the greatest reward is how these changes have strengthened our relationship.

The words, "You can never truly understand someone until you have walked a mile in their shoes" hold real meaning for us now!

The additions in our lives have been many but no bigger than Jimmy being given the opportunity to not only watch his daughters play soccer but to coach his oldest daughter's team. In another area of growth, as a couple we have consciously worked to find both old and new things we have in common and to build upon them. We know so many couples who, when the children leave home, suddenly find they live different lives and now have nothing in common. We don't want that to happen to us, but it easily could if we don't pay attention.

Lori remembers an aphorism that has been handed down in her family.

> **"Every couple must remember that you start your life together as two – with God's will your family will grow – and with God's will you will find yourselves as TWO once more."**

It is for this very reason that couples MUST continue to grow as a unit of two otherwise they may wake up one morning after the children leave home to find themselves living with a stranger.

We are growing as individuals and as a couple with each passing day, and sharing this with our children is very

important to us. By sharing these visions and dreams with our daughters we are letting them know that this is something we do. A very wise man named Gilbert, who we are blessed to have as a mentor, tells us on a regular basis: *"They do not do what you say... they do what you do."*

There are some skills that are best learned as a child; one that comes to mind is the art of dreaming. If you do not learn to dream as a child it will be very difficult to develop a vision of what you want your life to be as an adult. Having goals is important but one must be flexible with those goals when it comes to maintaining the relationships that are really important in your life. As the vision we have for our lives expands, it is a natural progression for our children to expand their ideas of what is possible for their lives. When we were so focused on rodeo, even though we did that as a family, they were exposed to mostly people from the rodeo world. Because we have expanded our circle, so has their circle grown. They now have the opportunity to meet and learn from a wide variety of people from different backgrounds. By expanding their horizons they will see diversity in the world and learn that there are always options out there – one just has to look for them.

It is the commitment we have to each other that gives us the strength to work through the challenges and changes that life throws our way. Foremost in our minds is our vision of setting a good example for our daughters. As parents we must come to accept that our children see what we do, what we say, and who we really are in the privacy of our own home, and they will emulate that in their lives; so once again, the key lies in our homes.

WORK VS. RELATIONSHIPS

In today's busy world it is easy to feel pulled in many different directions. The truth is that you can always do more at home or at work but there never seems to be enough time to do it all, being pulled in one direction by your partner and in what seems like the opposite direction by your boss. There are times, as in our case, when the demands of the farm and ranch business must take precedence. We have lived in this type of environment and have had different occupations, so we know the pressure and stress this can create from time to time.

The only cure is to set goals for yourself as to how much time you are going to spend at home and at work, taking into consideration what is really important to you. If you are trying to please others, such as your boss or your spouse, you will most likely feel stressed because both will want more from you than you can realistically give. Pleasing others ahead of pleasing yourself introduces a great deal of ongoing stress in people's lives. You have the power to choose how you spend your time and what affects you emotionally, so use it. It is not worth being miserable just to try and give someone else what they want.

However, often the real issue isn't spending too much time at work. Sometimes work can be an escape from home and sometimes home can be an escape from work. If you feel pressured and stressed about money, maybe you feel you should spend more time at work but don't really want to, and that can make you angry or frustrated. The same is true if you feel that your spouse wants you to stay at home all the time and not have any recreation without them. This can indicate an issue that

has nothing to do with your staying at home. These issues must be addressed before you can move forward in the relationship because saying nothing leaves everyone unsatisfied.

Many parents spend their time scurrying here and there, trying to get everything done. They always feel there isn't enough time and if they could just somehow speed up they might get it all done. We have learned that there is enough time without trying to squeeze every minute. If you focus all your attention on what you are doing and stop thinking about the other things that need to be done, you can enjoy your children and spouse while still getting things done.

For us it was about focusing first on the QUALITY; if it is family time, then our focus MUST be on the family. Our children aren't involved in every possible sport or activity. We want them to learn to choose and we also want to create time for the family. These days it seems like children are entertained every second of the day with DVDs, iPhones, videogames and many other gadgets. But this takes away from interacting with others, which is a very important lifeskill set that is falling through the cracks in today's society.

Sometimes the stress of parenthood can be overwhelming, but it's also true that the rewards are great. It is helpful and important for us to practice gratitude in our family. We all know people who have endured unspeakable tragedy in their lives. Instead of focusing on the negatives we try to remember how grateful we are to have each other, our children, our family, our friends, and our health. We believe that being grateful makes the tough times easier to face because you know how much you have!

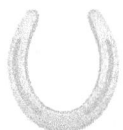

Every area of your life – your children, your home, your work – must complement each other to add to your overall happiness. Through work we gain feelings of accomplishment and success, as well as income to support the family. Through our family we get the emotional support that sustains us at work. The two became synergistic: work supports the family and the family supports work. At this stage of our lives, we are looking to blend work and fun so that it will be hard to tell when work ends and fun begins.

> *The greatest kind of work is when your*
> *work is your passion, because it fulfills you*
> *and allows the freedom to enjoy*
> *all that is precious in your life.*

TAKE RESPONSIBILITY

It is human nature not to want to be blamed or be at fault when something goes wrong. To avoid being blamed some people relinquish responsibility, even for their own lives. They act as though circumstances and conditions determine what happens in their lives rather than understanding that they have an active role in those circumstances and also have the power to change them. Rather than being at the center and in control of their lives, it is easier to blame conditions and circumstances. Feeling powerless, however, does not feel good. The only way to change what is happening in our lives is to take responsibility for our results. This includes our lives as parents. If your children consistently behave badly, you must take responsibility for that as well as commit to taking steps to correct it.

The moment responsibility is taken results change because the *mindset* has changed. By taking responsibility we become empowered and know that our thoughts determine our results. We know that we have the power to attract what we bring into our lives. If we dwell on our thoughts of what we don't want, we will subconsciously bring that into our lives.

As we discussed, the Paerto Principle, or 80/20 rule, states that 20% of the people in any field earn 80% of the money. That is because those 20% have replaced old beliefs and ideas with the awareness that they can actively improve their results by taking control of and responsibility for their lives. The 80% who are left to share the remaining 20% of the money are still allowing their old ideas to convince them that they are powerless against conditions and circumstances. Taking responsibility not only gives you the power to change your results; it also increases your self-respect. It encourages you to be creative and contribute to your own welfare and to the welfare of others.

The most important factor in our decision regarding anything we do is whether it will move our lives or our minds forward. If the answer is yes, we do it; if not, we don't. There is nothing more important than your self-respect and the image you have of yourself as an individual and as a couple. There is no greater stress than not feeling good about you.

In our journey to awareness, we came to the realization that we are filled with other people's ideas and beliefs. Our parents and their parents before them going back for several generations have each passed down their perceptions and ideas that were meant to guide and protect us. Many of these ideas were very

positive, such as knowing the value of honesty, integrity, and hard work. There have been issues to overcome but we are tackling these issues, where once we might have just ignored them or hoped they would go away. No more sticking our heads in the sand! We have learned that we have to be willing to address the problems before we can grow as people or grow in a relationship.

There are many individuals who blame various entities – the weather, the government, the economy – but none of these outside entities control your life. They don't determine what you do or do not believe in, or how you perceive events in your life. You do. You choose these things and you have the power to unchoose them as well. We may not be able to influence the weather, but we are totally in charge of our attitude about it.

In coming to appreciate that our thinking is what truly controls the results we have in our life, we are much more focused on changing ourselves to produce the outcomes we want. The quality of relationships with family, friends, and everyone we meet is clearly the result of our thinking. In changing old ideas we have certainly learned that education is not just learning new information; it is using what we learn to change our lives. We have accepted the fact that our present life and our relationships are the outcome of our thinking up to this moment. If we want them to change in any way we need to change our thoughts.

There have been times when we might have been afraid to pursue a dream or even have one for fear we would fail. It is easy to stop yourself from succeeding so as not to face possible disappointment. We follow the paradigms we have been taught as a way of protecting ourselves. Knowing that we will not pass on to our children the beliefs we change keeps us motivated.

We now realize that to accomplish something big, something worthy of our effort, we have to dream big and put all our energy and passion into that dream. We know we will not achieve our dreams by dreaming small and settling for less. Going through life like that stifles the passion and zest for life.

Thomas Edison tried hundreds of failed experiments on his way to inventing the light bulb. He took each outcome as feedback that he needed to proceed to his next experiment until he finally succeeded. In addition to his healthy acceptance of whatever results he got, Edison showed how necessary persistence is to achievement. He said: *"Genius is 1% inspiration and 99% perspiration."* Using feedback and persistence we can accomplish whatever we put our minds to.

Like Edison, we too can bring light into the darkness.

To dream big we need to recapture our imaginations. We had wonderful imaginations as children but our beliefs taught us not to follow them, to be reasonable and realistic – in other words, to lower our expectations and settle for less. We were taught to stop dreaming because *"adults don't dream; only children do."* We were also taught that we had to know how we were going to achieve a dream in order to pursue it. This is a deadly paradigm that will crush your imagination. We can immediately stop ourselves from pursing any goal by insisting that we need to know how we are going to accomplish it. The real challenge is to put your imagination to work to come up with your dream. Do not let yourself be stopped when you don't have the answer to the *'how.'* The how will come as you pursue your dream. Einstein said, *"Imagination is more important than intellect."* He knew how to dream big and look what he discovered!

The question we ask you to think about as you go forward is: *What would you do in your relationship right now if you knew you could not fail?* Dream big knowing you *cannot fail.* This is a change that involves only you doing something new. It does not require that your partner do something new. Whatever you do, you will not fail. You will get feedback to help you figure out your next step, but *you will not fail.* If your paradigms rise up to stop you, see them for what they are: paradigms, nothing more. You can choose to succeed in every area of life including your relationships. No matter how tattered and torn they may seem right now, changing the patterns in your life starts with changing your mind – and that is up to you.

"When the fabric of our relationships is spun of openness, love, and trust, then

In the silence between the words, the tapestry is made complete."

NINE

THE WORST HARD TIME

"Your LIFE is an occasion – Rise to it!"

CHAPTER 9

Hard times and failure are really states of mind. While you might argue this point, know that there are always those who are in worse situations than you will ever encounter and yet they *persevere* and *thrive*. The key to overcoming challenges and setbacks lies in changing your perception of those events and releasing your emotional attachment to them. Each person must realize that when something negative happens, they have the *choice* to let go of those emotions or to hold on to them, revisiting them in their mind until they can no longer move forward.

There are times when we all experience setbacks as individuals and as a family unit, no matter how far along the road we are or how successful we become. The key to getting past them is understanding how these events can affect our minds and what we can do about it.

With every long-term goal you set there will be challenges – some small, some HUGE! Most say that a setback or two along the way to a particular goal is a good thing, and that has been our experience. This is because it forces us to develop the

character to persevere and even more importantly it gives us an opportunity to grow as a person. Being challenged in life is inevitable but being defeated is a *choice*. When our ideas are challenged and questioned by others it forces us to evaluate them and ensure that we are on the right path for us. Even when we are convinced our idea is a great one, possibly even life changing, people may still reject it, forcing us to go it alone. This is when each of us must take a look inside ourselves and decide if we are going to set our OWN path in life or follow the path that others have set for us! You must determine your own results – do not play it safe and settle for the mediocre results of others.

When Edison was working on inventing the light bulb the masses saw the idea as *"dumb."* We now have the privilege of hindsight to see the courage and perseverance he had to bring us one of the greatest inventions of the last century. What we must all realize is that even when ideas have a proven track record such as the "light bulb," there will still be people who reject it! This is proof that even when you see the possibilities and potential of a project, there will be others that will only see the *risk* and potential *downside*. If we always evaluate the validity of negative opinions, we will stay on the right track and not allow someone else's constant negativity to defeat us. This can be especially difficult within a family. When one person grows and moves forward while another does not, the fear of being left behind takes hold. The natural tendency of humans is to pull back the person who is moving ahead, thinking and wanting to believe that we are *'saving'* them from the unknown; but in reality all we are doing is stopping them from moving

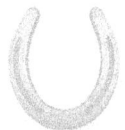

ahead of us. As with most things in a family, you have to balance your goals by setting good boundaries so you can accomplish what you want in life while still encouraging other family members and friends to come along with you rather than pull you backwards.

We have all been taught that failure is bad; this could not be further from the truth. Failure needs to be seen as a course correction, nothing more. We would never expect to get on a horse the first time and ride like an expert, yet we approach life with this perfectionist attitude, thinking that if we cannot do something perfectly then we shouldn't even try. The healthier approach is to see setbacks and failures as the temporary by-products of creativity. In order for each of us to move forward, there will be the occasional misstep, but it doesn't erase all we've gained by taking the journey. To be a real winner in life we have to understand failure and learn to tolerate the temporary agony it produces because we know things will get better. Real winners understand that the knowledge gained from experience is valuable in improving their lives. Anyone who is willing to take a *risk* and *lose* will eventually achieve *success.*

So what if your grand idea fails miserably, what then? You learned a lot and this information will help you get it right and succeed. No high achiever has arrived without many failures. It is easy to see successful people and assume that it was easy for them. Most of the time, people who have achieved 'overnight' success have worked for years in obscurity to achieve their goals. J.K. Rowling, author of the now famous Harry Potter books, spent more than 10 years getting rejection after

rejection from publishers, who were convinced that children would never read a book more than 400 pages long, nor would they understand plots as complex as the ones she wrote. She persevered and time proved her right and the 'experts' wrong. Yet if you had asked her at year number eight how successful she was, she might have responded that she was a big fat failure because at that point she'd had nothing but negative feedback; still, she picked herself up and kept going – that is what it takes to be a *success*.

It's Everyone Else's Fault

Our first reaction when things don't go our way is to blame anyone or anything but ourselves. When we perceive others are to blame, then there is nothing we can do to correct the problem. This attitude of blame is the easy way out because it allows us to escape taking any responsibility for the problem. By not taking responsibility we allow ourselves to feel it is not our responsibility to fix the problem. As a result we do nothing and continue to tell ourselves it's someone else's fault – thus setting up a cycle of complaining and griping about everything except the real problem.

The only way to break the cycle of blame is to assume responsibility – even when it is easier to blame others. Only when we take that first courageous step to assume responsibility can we analyze what went wrong and take corrective action. We can't always choose or control the events that happen in our lives, but we can absolutely choose how we respond. This

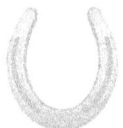

is another thing that Real Winners have – the art of bouncing back from failure.

There is no doubt that negative events are discouraging. They will drain your energy and possibly your resources but we cannot lose track of what they bring us: the knowledge of what to do next time to get things right. Perseverance is the greatest knowledge given; it is what separates those who think they want success from those who are determined to have it, to *WIN*. Once you decide to keep going, the playing field will narrow and it will get easier.

In most cases, all blaming others does is give us the "OK" to quit – a way out. When we quit, it is important to determine whether we did so because we were going in the wrong direction or because we gave up. One way to make this determination is to abandon the project or put it to rest for a time. When the mind is free of pressures, realistic planning emerges. It is important to realize that this time is not wasted; it is of great benefit; it is the art of redirection. When you try again, chances are you will get it right. New outlooks are the result of surviving failure. The strong learn to hang in there and keep bouncing back until they win.

"Real Winners"

People who accept the belief that they are failures are easily controlled. We see this everywhere in our world and sometimes this is perpetuated in families. Years ago, parents used the motivation tool of reward and punishment to

motivate their children. The intent was to motivate them to co-operate; instead all it did was remind people of their failures. Disciplinary action means internal motivation has not worked and external motivation has been reverted to. With children this can be extremely damaging, as a self-fulfilling prophecy takes over and they become convinced that they can't succeed. We as parents have a choice in how we raise our children, and parenting, just like many other aspects of life, takes perseverance and learning. No one starts out being a perfect parent or perfect spouse; we learn as we go and inevitably will make mistakes, but it's never too late to correct those errors and get on the right path.

Sometimes getting the support of others is as simple as supporting and believing in yourself. Often we give lip service to believing in ourselves, but our words and actions betray our real feelings. We are constantly sending out unconscious signals to the people around us as to how we feel deep down about our own abilities.

Believe it or not, you could be the cause of your own lack of results. We do and say things habitually and if we never gain the awareness that there might be a better way, we continue to repeat these patterns. How often do you do things for your children because it is faster and easier than taking the time to teach them or allow them to fail at something? We all do this but you must become aware that this only robs them of valuable learning experiences they will need later in life. How often do you complain to your spouse that he or she didn't do something as well as you expected? This happens all the time and the result is usually that your spouse will no longer try

and you become overloaded with things that only you can do 'correctly.' Or do you send them a message that shows your lack of self-confidence, and then get angry when they agree?

Check yourself closely to see what kind of signals you are sending to your loved ones. Do you find yourself voicing a plan to begin something and use words and statements that imply doubt on your part? For example: *"I'm going to try this and see how it goes."* Or, *"I sure hope this new idea of mine works out."* These statements will not WIN their support.

Giving support to a friend or loved one is a commitment on the part of the person giving the support. Therefore the one asking for the support must be firmly committed to the project that they want support for. Check carefully and become aware of your behavior and the words you use. Once you remove all doubt about your own commitment to your plans, you will gain more support.

THE COMFORT ZONE

"Change is the LAW of LIFE.
And those who look only to the past or present
– are certain to miss the FUTURE."

–John F. Kennedy
President of the United States

It is human nature to take *RISKS* – so why do so few of us do so? *"Conditioning"* – over the years, our environment has been conditioning us to "play *it safe.*" While our innate nature needs to test the limits and grow, our belief systems attempt

to convince us that this is bad, resulting in inaction. The more conditioned we are by people and things around us, the bigger challenge we face to break away.

Your *comfort zone* is the lifestyle that you have become accustomed to. It is where you feel safe and *"comfortable."* Anyone who has studied physics knows that it takes much more energy to get an object moving than it does to keep it moving. Once we fall into our personal *comfort zone,* we stop moving. We get used to our surroundings and actively choose not to leave. We reason that it's better to play to it safe than step out into the great unknown out of our *"box."* We worry about what other people will think about us if we *risk* and *fail.*

> *Where would we be today if our forefathers stayed in their comfort zone? If they hadn't taken huge risks and come to the New World or out West?*

We have learned not to worry so much about what other people think. As a matter of fact, it doesn't matter what other people think. Most of the time they don't really think at all, and in many cases they are just repeating the preconceived ideas and training they received throughout their lives. Most people are reflecting where they currently are in their lives and it has nothing to do with you or where you want to go.

We now understand that risk is natural, and to risk intelligently is what we are supposed to do to have a fulfilling life. The key is to be more consciously aware and to ignore the external forces that hinder us and push us off track. It took a shift

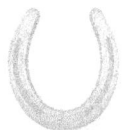

in our thought process to create enough desire to move beyond the safety of what we were used to – what we used to be.

Have you ever asked a group of people, *"If you had your life to live all over again, what would you do different?"* We have and we received many answers such as, *"I would have married my high school sweetheart,"* or *"I would have spent more time with my children."* Then we asked a more specific question, *"When you were faced with a decision that involved risk, the kind that made you uncomfortable and took courage to act upon, what did you do?"* Few replied that they took on the challenge, while most replied that they did not act and reverted to safety.

> *"You'll seldom experience regret for anything that you've done. It is what you haven't done that will torment you."*
>
> –WAYNE DYER
> AUTHOR/SPEAKER

Lori remembers this all too well.

When her Grandpa passed away, her Dad asked if she wanted to do the eulogy. She did but was scared – what if she broke down and cried in front of all those people? These feelings were supported; rather than responding, "What does that matter?" Her family said, "It's okay, we know how hard it would be for you – you have not seen some of the people who will be at the funeral for years." All of these people were looking out for her because they did not want to see her fail at something that was very important to her.

Lori says it was her biggest regret because she didn't even try – her Grandpa Walter had meant so much to her and she felt like she let him down. So when her Grandma passed away a few years later, she simply informed her parents that she was doing the eulogy and if one of the other grandchildren wanted to join, she would love it.

It was the hardest thing she has ever done but also the most rewarding. Tears held off until the end but that did not matter because she had done what she had come to do. Tears are only feelings and need to be shared more often, not placed behind a mask. She knew that day that both her Grandma and Grandpa were smiling down on her with pride because she had faced her fear. Standing there with her cousin was hard but something that the two of them will share forever! (Thanks, Stacy)

Those who risked all said they were glad – they had no regrets. They also said they wished they had risked more and earlier in their lives. Those who stayed within their *comfort zone* – their *"box"* – wished for a second chance to jump at the opportunity and to take that *risk*. The regret for these people was so great that we could see it in their body language and facial expressions. For many, we believe that hindsight *"kicked in"* once they saw that the world of uncertainty was actually not that scary or risky after all. It only *appeared* to be risky due to their self-limiting beliefs and other peoples' beliefs which they accepted as their own. It was hard for these people to look back and realize they would have in all probability accomplished much more and led more fulfilled lives had they taken a few more *RISKS*.

If you see or find a worthy goal that you want to accomplish, there will always be a certain uneasiness that you feel. When you are not used to taking risks your mind will respond negatively. It is much like when you take a child for their first haircut. Though it is completely harmless, the uncertainty often makes children cry or even near hysterical! Our adult minds react in this same way when we contemplate something we've never tried before. It is like a tug of war that takes place in the mind. *Fear vs. Risk.* Fear may attempt to stop you; it is totally up to you if you allow it to or NOT!

What each of us has to accept is that in any endeavor, one can always find reasons why it is not wise. But by the same measure, if you search for and focus on the rewards, your mind will find plenty of benefits. This is why it is so important to *focus* on the *rewards*. The more you hold the *images* of the *reward* in your *mind*, the more you *silence* that inner *fear*.

> *"A CHAMPION is someone*
> *who gets up when he can't."*
>
> –JACK DEMPSEY
> WORLD HEAVY WEIGHT BOXER

The truth of the matter is you can have fear without risk, but you can't have risk without fear. The very basis of risk is that it is something that scares us and this fear in years past was helpful to keep us out of physical danger. With this understanding, know that *fear* is *natural* and even healthy, as long as it does not paralyze. You can even use fear as your ally.

Use it in such a manner that it compels you to do your due diligence and research. However, also realize that the stars will never line up perfectly. If you are waiting for this, you will be saying "*if only I would have*" many years from now. After you've done your homework, you must trust your intuition and take decisive action.

When taking intelligent risks, you will find that the results justify the risks and once those goals are met, your perception changes and you view those risks as small rather than large. The challenge most people have is that they have an aversion to risk that seems hard to overcome. However, this aversion is not natural; it is learned. We have been conditioned since birth to "take the safe route" and that it's "better to be safe than sorry."

Think back to when you were a young child or observe babies today; risk is embraced and a natural part of their being. When you were a child, you thought big. Your ideas were big. You thought you could do anything. As children, the word "impossible" did not exist in our vocabulary.

Ten foot tall and bulletproof.

But as we got older, most of us were overwhelmed by outside influences, stifling this natural urge to *risk*. Now, most of us must struggle to overcome this conditioning in every area of our lives.

If we really want rich rewards in all areas of our lives, we cannot follow the crowd. We must be uncommon in our philosophy and approach. Nothing is impossible if backed by

a definite *desire* and *purpose* for what you want in your life. Risk is not the issue. As our desire and passion increase, what may appear as *"risk"* to an outsider is really not risk at all; it is moving forward with confidence and decisive action as we visualize the *rewards* that await us.

"You miss one hundred percent of the shots you don't take."

—WAYNE GRETZKY
NHL HOCKEY PLAYER

OVERCOMING WITH GRATITUDE

"Develop an attitude of gratitude, and give thanks for everything that happens to you, knowing that every step forward is a step toward achieving something bigger."

—BRIAN TRACY
AUTHOR/SPEAKER

Part of a successful attitude and lifestyle is the ability to give back to your community, to your family, and to others who seek to learn what you know. While we are far from where we want to be, part of the reason we wrote this book was to share with others what we've learned to this point. We are a great example that your life need not be perfect to move forward and help others and you can do this too.

As you achieve greater and great heights, you may notice that the goals that you set have more to do with moving others

forward rather than yourself. This is a natural result of living a happier lifestyle. It becomes second nature to uplift others and help them find their way. You honor those who helped you by concentrating your efforts on those that you can now help.

Looking back, Jimmy now knows it was time to take a step back in rodeo – not to leave behind a sport he loved, but to find a way to give back. He does this by helping others who want to move up to the professional ranks by sharing what he has learn along the trail.

Whenever you shift your perspective from yourself to others, energy increases and conditions for success reveal themselves in the form of unexpected opportunities and results. This includes a movement on your part away from anger, stinginess, and hurt feelings toward generosity. Even the smallest movement in that direction can attract sudden good fortune to you.

A related way to attract sudden good fortune is to feel goodwill and gratitude towards others. We believe giving is absolutely essential if we ever want to be truly prosperous and live a life of joy. Please bear in mind that giving is more about the act and process of giving, not the thing given. Besides money, giving can also be the giving of your time, the giving of a compliment, or a simpe smile to a stranger.

You and you alone are totally responsible for your life. You and you alone are totally responsible for your peace of mind. All the money in the world will not give you peace. No other person – your spouse, your children, your friends – can give you peace. Running to teachers for answers will not give you peace. Moving to a different location will not give you peace.

None of these will give you peace because peace does not come from outside sources. It can only be obtained by looking within. The answers that you long for are already a part of you. You have only to understand and practice them; only then will you lead a peaceful and happy existence.

If you give peace and love to everyone you know and meet, no matter how they treat you, you will receive peace and love in return. If you are hateful, full of hatred and cruelty, cruel and terrible people will enter your life.

Attaining peace is as simple as this: *Give peace and you will receive peace.*

People start early in life with the attitude of revenge and this is often learned from those around us. Anger is an immature attitude but one we do not outgrow. When a child becomes angry at another child for breaking a toy, they have not yet learned to be tolerant and understanding. The child's first reaction is to hit back and break the other child's toy. As we enter adulthood fully developed and mature, we need to learn to be tolerant of the mistakes of others and forgive mistakes in order to grow as an individual. Most of us understand that a fight does not begin until the second person strikes back.

> *It is your choice to go there,*
> *and your choice to walk away.*

How often does a person truly give without the thought of something in return? When you give love you expect love in return. When you give understanding to someone you expect

them to be understanding in return. When you give a gift you usually expect a gift back and you expect that the person will like you or respect you more for having given them a gift. Few give just to give.

When a person does not return exactly what we expected or perhaps even more, the tendency is to feel hurt or even hostile and angry. What we fail to realize is that all people have *choices*. They are individuals just as we are. Because different people are motivated by different things, they will not respond in exactly the way we might want them to respond. It takes little effort to love and give to those who give love in return.

The rewards in life are not measured by how much a person can gain cheating on their income taxes or by how much they can hurt others. The rewards come from how much can be given to assist others. The rewards you will gain by being a giver are true peace and a feeling of beautiful wholeness. When you stop worrying about what the other person thinks of you and start being concerned about what you think of yourself, this is when you will grow in understanding.

We hope our words will help you neutralize your past negative feelings, capture your feelings for the right reasons, and become a person that you can love and respect, and thus you will be loved and respected by others.

> *"The people who receive the most
> are the ones who give the most."*

–SUSAN BAGYURA
AUTHOR

TEN

HAPPINESS IS THE JOURNEY

*"Every decision you make – every decision
– is not a decision about what to do.*

It's a decision about WHO YOU ARE.

*When you see this, when you understand it,
everything changes.*

You begin to see in a new way.

*All events, occurrences, and situations turn into
opportunities to do what you came here to do."*

—NEALE DONALD WALSCH
AUTHOR

CHAPTER 10

The one thing that has become *"crystal clear"* in our minds is that life will only be as great as you *choose* for it to be. We have realized that what we think, how we feel, and how we react to any given situation or event is totally within our control. The hard truth is the only limits in our lives are those we place on ourselves. If you want to change, you have to make the decision to change and the change will start with making the simpe *choice* to be open to CHANGE! The life you dreamed of can be yours – if you belief it can! The fact that you may not believe this is exactly what is holding you back. All you need to do is allow yourself to start dreaming again and believe that wonderful things can come into your life.

We think one of the most rewarding aspects of the process of recreating your life is that it will renews the childlike excitement you once had when you knew your life stretched out before you. No matter your age, there is still a lot of life to live, and the best part is that it's all waiting for you to come and get it. The first step is to take some time to seriously evaluate where you currently are in every aspect of your life. The next most exhilarating, exciting step is to start dreaming about what you really want in regards to finances, relationships, health, and family time.

It is extremely important to be very honest about where you are in life because this is what will form the basis for creating a path of where your want to go. This whole exercise will allow you to see what you want and determine what that *'more'* looks like to you. The one thing we have come to realize is that "*more*" is individual to each of us. Once you know what "*more*" is to you, you can define exactly what you want to be and how you want your life to unfold. The reward is that you will be *CHOICING* your life rather than just accepting the life that others have envisioned for you. Grab all the drama that life throws your way and get excited about all that is possible. The life you envision is yours to create. As you grow and change, so will your dreams and goals. Right now you may just want a different job or to relocate or to reconnect with family. As you reach each goal, you are FREE to envision the next goal. Each goal achieved will give you the POWER to dream BIGGER! Wanting more is human nature. The key is to have BALANCE in all that you DREAM!

For example, we thought that when we purchased the family ranch we would have more balance and stability in our life. The reality was that all we got was more time lost with a huge increase in financial uncertainty. Most people see our industry as one where the producer is in control; that could not be farther from the truth; it is controlled by BIG business, like most industries in our country. The truth is that more and more farms and ranches require an off ranch/farm job or business to support a LIFESTYLE. We realized we did not just want to make a living;

we wanted to live. *If we continued on the same path we would not be further ahead in twenty years. This life changing discovery made us sit down and refocus. We had to determine where we wanted to be in twenty years and how we could get there and maintain balance in our life. The first step was to get what we owned to work for us rather than us working for it! This was a hard time for our family, filled with a lot of ups and downs, but we knew we had to reinvent ourselves. We can honestly say that the hard times are where the growth happens because these are the times we must reevaluate ourselves and what we really want.*

The first step for each of us who wants to change our quality of life is to accept that where we are right now is the result of all the *choices* we have made in the past. It is important to understand how the power to choose helps us make the decisions that turn our dreams into reality. Once we accept responsibility for our circumstances, we can follow these steps to help make the changes that will ultimately lead us to success.

1. GET CLEAR ON WHAT YOU REALLY WANT

"Everything begins with an IDEA."

– EARL NIGHTINGALE
AUTHOR/RADIO COMMENTATOR

If you do not understand where you are going, your life could be characterized as running through a dark forest and hoping for the best. When you focus and plan for what you want, you stay moving in the right direction. Dreams are best met when they are fully developed in your mind. Make your

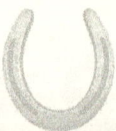

goals so clear you can see them and more importantly feel them. Visualize the outcome and imagine how your life will be when it happens. As you move along in your quest, you must stop on occasion to see if your vision is still clear. If it is fuzzy, you will still need to further refine or possibly start off in a new direction. This is why putting your goals in writing is so very important. It allows you to see what you want on a daily basis and reminds you of how far you've come.

2. POSITIVE REINFORCEMENT

"Every achiever that I have ever met says, 'My life turned around when I began to BELIEVE in me.'"

–DR ROBERT SCHULLER
MINISTER/AUTHOR

Once you have defined what you want in great detail, use positive reinforcement to keep the goals clear and focused in your mind. Positive thoughts are extremely powerful. They will help you shift your focus from *"I can't"* or *"I'm afraid"* to *"I can"* and *"I will."* The key is to use words or phrases that help you picture what it is you want to achieve. Be specific, keep your words in the first person, and stay positive. For example: "I am surrounded by people who value and respect me for who I am and what I do." By affirming your goals clearly in your mind, you are sending your subconscious a message that will support and encourage you. All of this will keep you tuned into your goal and be aware of all the opportunities around you that will help you achieve your goal.

3. FOCUSED INTENT

> *"The major reason for setting a goal is what it makes you do to accomplish it.*
>
> *What it makes of you will always be the far greater value that what you get."*
>
> –JIM ROHN
> ENTREPRENEUR/AUTHOR/SPEAKER

There is one thing that all successful people are: they are motivated people who stay focused on their *goals*. Successful people keep their goals constantly in front of them and take specific, measurable steps to work toward these goals each day. We cannot say it enough; you get what you think about; what you focus on is what you bring into your life. When you have a *'crystal clear'* vision, you become aware of what is relevant to your life or business and you will attract the opportunities that will help you have the life you dream about.

4. ACTION

> *"Change is inevitable, personal growth is a choice."*
>
> – BOB PROCTOR
> AUTHOR/SPEAKER

The first step to your new life is making a decision, but nothing will happen unless you take *action*. You must commit to actions that will move you towards your goal. Start with

making the decision to complete one step (even if it's a small step) each day that moves you toward your *goals*.

We started by making a list of five things that we must accomplish the next day – we made the commitment to make a plan ahead of time. You might think this takes a lot of time but it can usually be accomplished with a commitment of less than 30 minutes per day once you have a 'crystal clear' vision of where you want to go. Make a list of the five items you want to accomplish the next day and work to achieve them each day. Finish each item before you move on to the next. It is important to understand that quality is better than quantity. You can accomplish more in 30 minutes of focusing than you can in a whole afternoon when your mind wanders from your current task to the next on the list.

5. KEEPING YOUR ATTITUDE IN CHECK

> *"I am determined to be cheerful and happy in whatever situation I may find myself.*
>
> *For I have learned that the greater part of our misery or unhappiness is determined not by our circumstance but by our disposition."*
>
> —MARTHA WASHINGTON
> FIRST AMERICAN FIRST LADY

Your *attitude* is one area that you must control at all times. Your *attitude* not only affects how you approach your goals, but it also determines your perspective of past events. The way we view ourselves determines our perspective on life. A positive

mental attitude enhances your feelings of empowerment and makes it possible to continue moving forward even when problems and obstacles appear.

There are times when we all need a good laugh, and we all know that a few minutes of humor can dispel hours of frustration. So please do not miss an opportunity to laugh at yourself – especially when you're taking things way too seriously. When challenges threaten to completely overwhelm you, it is a good time to step back emotionally and give yourself a break. Take 30 minutes away from the challenge and do something you enjoy. When we give our mind time to relax, our emotions are set free and the result is that you can return to those challenges with renewed energy and concentration. With each problem that you overcome, your self-confidence will be boosted. The result will be that whenever you find yourself thinking negative thoughts, you will stop yourself immediately and replace those thoughts with positive ideas.

6. PERSISTENCE

"You can achieve anything you want in life if you have the courage to DREAM it, the intelligence to make a realistic PLAN, and the DESIRE to see that plan through to the end."

— SIDNEY A. FRIEDMAN
ENTREPRENEUR/SPEAKER/AUTHOR

There will be times that you feel like you are a hamster on a wheel never really getting anywhere – certainly not any closer to your goal. All we can say is 'don't get discouraged'; it will happen. Though it may seem like you aren't making progress, you are. You are learning and growing as a person with each tiny step, and those same steps are gathering steam to push you through to that goal. Hard-won goals are the most rewarding and satisfying. Over time you will notice that you're accomplishing more with less effort. Things get a little easier. Situations don't frustrate you like they used to and this comes from having the courage to keep trying and not give up.

Refuse to allow unhelpful criticism or negative circumstances to sway you from your goals. No matter the road you travel in life, it is all about the journey, so allow yourself to enjoy it. A successful life isn't a destination; it is a state of being that exists every day. The work you do, the people you meet, and the experiences you have along the way to meeting your goals are what makes your life fulfilled and happy. Let your mind unlock all the possibilities.

When you are living the quality of life you choose then you have more to give to others; more to give emotionally, financially, and more time to share. It is your responsibility and privilege to raise your quality of life so you can support other people in raising theirs. Can you imagine a world where everyone is being their best and able to encourage all they meet to be their best as well? When you raise the quality of your life you will be an integral part of making this world a better place and you will be a better person for it.

THE JOYFUL LIFE

*"Gratitude is not only the greatest virtue,
but the parent of all others."*

—CICERO
PHILOSOPHER

Ask yourself: *"Am I grateful for the life I have right now?."*
We caution you not to confuse being grateful with having
everything you want. As human beings, we are created to
always want, to be more and do more. That being said, you
may possibly not be all that happy about what you've created
so far, and that's okay. We now know that it is the pain we have
experienced that has allowed us to recognize the joyful times
in our life and be grateful for those times. Each of us knows
someone who has been rejected or abandoned and who has
gone through more hurt than any human should have to. The
truth is that because of these painful experiences these people
develop a greater love and learn to care more deeply and have
greater compassion for others. When we look back at it as part
of the journey, it will be a source of great strength and power
rather than an excuse to be miserable.

The most powerful thing in life is to be grateful for whatever
you have right now. When you are grateful for what you have
you will attract into your life more things to be grateful for, and
you will be joyous in the process. It is a wonderful exercise to
take inventory of how many things you have to be grateful for.
Write them down, track them, and make a game to see if you

can come up with additional things over time. Notice how you feel while engaged in this action. Try it when you are waiting in the long line at the bank or the grocery store. Observe what effect your joyful state has on the people around you. You may never know what difference you made in someone's life just by sharing a simple smile. Think of how a simple smile from someone else makes you feel.

Joyfulness is a state of mind. It is a choice. You choose joy just like you decide what clothes you will wear today. The saddest thing is that so many people don't allow themselves to feel joy and fewer go out and share it with others. By making it a top priority in your family you will have an enormous affect on the world around you. Some people who are close to you may not understand the changes you are making and might question you for your joyful attitude. They might even make fun of you. It's at those times that you will need to draw on what you are grateful for – we call it our mind shifting list. What difference can you make in their lives by truly caring and sharing your joyous spirit with them? When we are joyful and we share our joyous spirit with those around us – we show we care. It is said that people do what we do, not what we say, so show them a joyful life is possible; give them hope. Always remember that the choice, of course, will always be theirs, but invite them to join you in feeling true joy about life.

Have you ever noticed your mood change because you were listening to someone else complaining?

We listened one evening while a man was complaining about his irritation with some family member. He went on and on for a while. When he was done we noticed that we were now in a

grumpy mood because he had just dumped his garbage onto us. It was incredibly powerful to notice how being around someone who was complaining had such a huge effect on the mood of everyone around him. Examples such as these have made each of us more aware of the effect we have on those around us. Each day we must be aware and do all we can to remove this kind of negativity from our home. When we talk about our tough experiences, we try to come up with solutions or a different perspective instead of bringing each other down. It is our affirmation to learn what we can from these experiences, to deal with them, and most importantly to "MOVE ON." We all must eliminate the habit of complaining for nothing good can or will ever come from it.

There are several different ways of finding and experiencing joy in your life. The first and perhaps most important is to know your purpose. Nothing will bring you joy more than knowing what you were meant to accomplish in your life. Not knowing can bring sadness, wondering, fear, and lack of fulfillment. Above all, find out what your unique purpose is here on this earth – then fulfill it. As you do, you will experience joy because you have found your true passion.

It is one thing to know your purpose, but then you need to live according to that purpose. This is a matter of priorities. Let your actions and schedule reflect your purpose. Don't react to circumstances and let them cause you to live without fulfilling that purpose. This will only result in frustration, anger, and bitterness, while living your purpose will bring you deep satisfaction and joy. Rather than settling for the status quo and letting life drift by, strive toward the higher goals and purpose.

Almost everyone knows someone who is a 'taker.' In order to have real joy in your life it is important to give more than you take. True joy lies in giving. While you can find a certain amount of happiness in accumulating material possessions, it will be a hollow gratification. Whether it is money, time, or just taking time to be kind, giving stays with you for a long time; buying stuff to make yourself feel better is fleeting and temporary.

So how do you bring joy into your life if you're not in the mood for it? Can you just fake it? Can you have joy on demand? Many people have legitimate reasons for being somewhat despondent, and when you're in that state of mind, how can you become joyful? You encounter people during the course of daily living who are joyous naturally and others that seemingly are much more somber and serious.

The opposite of joy is sadness, and these emotions are forces in our lives that have a very strong impact. If you saw the movie, *Patch Adams*, then you know how laughter can aid in healing. Joy is one of the most underused tools; by learning how to access it you will help yourself on a daily basis in every area of your life.

People often feel as if they are victims of circumstances. If something in our daily life brings us some joy we are grateful for it, but is there something that we can actually do that can help us bring joy all the time?

We've heard some people wonder if joy is genetic. You do find people who are just naturally joyous, who have a kind of laid back attitude where it's just good to be in their presence. Then there are other people in our lives who no matter how

upbeat we are, an encounter with them always bring us down. It is not genetic; it is inherited; we only have to observe children to know this is true. Before children have been affected by society, parents, and community, they can show us what life could be like. Children have natural cheer and excitement. They have a natural, enchanted air about them; some would call it innocence because they haven't yet tasted of the pains of life. We choose to say that it is a natural state that we all have within us.

Children cease to be consistently cheerful when life happens. Life changes for them with that first disappointment, their first grief, or their first loss. In other words, joy is a completely natural state. Because we live in a world with so much grief and pain, it is shocking to us to see someone who is joyous. So a child's innocence serves them well because they haven't yet tasted what it means to live in a world of deception. Once they experience those disappointments, the joy bottles up to the point that it is difficult to access again.

It is critical for us to put some perspective on this natural state. If happiness was an *acquired* state, something that you develop at some point (later) in life, then a very strong argument can be made that once you've lost a reason to be happy or you've suffered grief, there's no way of rekindling that joy.

However joy must be seen as a natural state of feeling, a certain sense of belonging, a feeling within that you are important and that you have value. When joy is seen in this light, the only question that needs to be asked is: "How does one reclaim that emotion?" Joy and happiness are things

that each of us has in our hearts already. Even if you are the saddest person and you haven't smiled in years, you have a joy, a gladness in your heart that may in some way be blocked or sealed because you may not feel that there's any reason to access it – but it's there.

Many personal development gurus and psychologists talk about your 'inner child.' The inner child has always been a reality and the concept is essentially that the natural cheer, the natural spirituality, the enchantment and magic of child life is maintained throughout our lives. The bad thing is that once we mature into adults, our lives harden and we lock that child up within us. When we lock the child up we lose that cheer, the natural happiness and joy of childhood. Our happiness and joy is determined by accessing and bringing back these qualities into our lives.

Take a look around at any particular situation and ask yourself when and why people are happy. Usually, there are a few ingredients that contribute to that happiness. Ingredient number one is that they feel needed and a vital part of the process. They feel appreciated that they're doing their job; they don't feel negligible; they don't feel taken advantage of; they feel that they belong and that their particular talents or strengths are being utilized and appreciated.

This type of inner security leads to natural joy. Indeed, inner security is essentially one and the same with inner joy. Natural joy doesn't mean you get up to dance and celebrate at every moment; it's a certain feeling that you are wanted and needed. And when you have that, you have no reason to be sad.

As you grow as a person and create the life you want, you naturally share that with those around you, including your children and family. You can look forward to leaving them a legacy of fulfillment and happiness – an example for what their lives can become. Once you change the course of your own life, it ripples out like circles in a pond touching untold numbers of lives for the better.

We encourage you to start your own journey now and use the techniques and ideas we have presented as a way to make your own ripples in life. You will in turn be leaving those you love the tremendous gift of hope that their lives will be as full and happy as the life you have created for yourself.

We want to leave you with a story that has touched us and given us something to focus on during the struggles of our journey.

There was a businessman who brought some work home with him. When he arrived home, his five-year-old son was ready to play. The Dad kept saying, "I have so much to do for work – maybe later." The boy just keep asking; the father kept answering his questions, and then the father came up with an idea. He found a magazine picture of the world, ripped it into pieces, and handled it to his son. "Put this picture together, son, and when you are done we can play." Dad thought that would buy him 20 to 30 minutes.

When his son returned only a few minutes later, the father was shocked. "How did you do that so fast?" The boy answered with a big smile on his face: "There was a man on the other side – when I got the man right, the world was right."

So remember as you work towards your dreams:

"Get you right and the right world
for you will follow."

That is all we want for you and it is our hope that this books helps you along your journey to your destiny!

Love, Jimmy & Lori

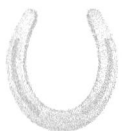